Dec 2016

To Aunt Katherine
& Uncle Bill

Love
Chris

Detecting the Gleam of Light
Thoughts for the Aspiring Creative Writer

Christine Mary McGinley

Detecting the Gleam of Light
Thoughts for the Aspiring Creative Writer

By Christine Mary McGinley

Copyright @ 2017 by Christine Mary McGinley

Book design by Agent 99 Design

All rights reserved. No part of this book may be reproduced or transmitted in any form or by any means, electronic or mechanical, including photocopying, recording, or by any information storage and retrieval system, without permission in writing from the publisher.

ISBN: 978-0-9972204-1-4

Library of Congress Control Number: 2016915763

Published by Gleam of Light Press LLC
P.O. Box 42
Lakeland, Michigan 48143 U.S.A.

www.GleamofLightPress.com

Printed in the United States of America

"A man should learn to detect and watch that gleam of light which flashes across his mind from within."

Ralph Waldo Emerson

Ralph Waldo Emerson
(1803—1882)

This book began as a book about creative writing. As the process took on a life of its own it became a book about a special kind of creative writing, which can only be called "Emersonian," as it is Emerson who has guided this process throughout.

Though this process too was a creative one, "scholarly" only in the Emersonian sense, it owes a tremendous debt to the many scholars who have devoted lifetimes to understanding Emerson. I acknowledge them with a full heart and have cited a number of them and their important works wherever their thoughts have better expressed my own.

Detecting the Gleam of Light will perhaps be of value to few aspiring writers. As I have thought about who you are, these are the qualities that have come to me: You would say of yourself, "I have always wanted to write." You feel you must write. And perhaps most important, when you open a book to read, what you are most hoping to find are ideas. Ideas that ignite something in you and make you feel more alive. Ideas that remind you that the sharing of ideas is your ultimate dream, your ultimate destiny.

The Yearning to Write	*1*
What is Creative Writing?	*5*
Creative Reading	*9*
Who is Emerson?	*13*
Reading Emerson	*27*
Self-Reliance	*41*
The Gleam of Light	*55*
Becoming a Writer	*67*
Finding Your Voice	*77*
Shutting Out the Other Voices	*87*
Tilling Your Plot of Ground	*99*
Word by Word	*113*
"The Soul's Emphasis is Always Right"	*125*
Aim High	*135*
The Process is the Prize	*145*

The Yearning to Write

I have known few people who have not at some time thought about writing. I would not be surprised to learn that most Americans some time in their lives experience the pangs of an aspiring writer. If you are one of these people I must tell you from the start that I have little to offer you on the subject of how to write, and even less on how to become a successful writer. The most important thing I have to tell you on both of these fronts is that it is thinking about these two things that most gets in the way for people who want to write.

As any serious writer will tell you, there is no one who can tell you how to write. This is something we must each discover on our own. And there is only one way to do this and that is to write. Anything a writer has to say about writing comes entirely from her own experience. Speak to another writer, you will perhaps hear very different things. There is one important beginning however that I believe every writer would agree on and that is reading. Read everything you love and only what you love. And then one day, and only in the moment when you feel you must, begin your own writing. Write for as long as it takes to have something you enjoy reading, something that compels you to keep working on what you have written. This is the beginning for any writer.

If your desire to write is accompanied by fantasies about producing bestsellers and being a "success" — well, those imaginings are difficult to avoid. None of us ever creates anything that we do not hope will one day be appreciated by great numbers of people. This is certainly part of what drives the creative process, the desire to reach others with our own thoughts and ideas. What we all need to understand, whatever kind of writing we wish to do, is that there are very few successful writers in the world. By this I mean people who write exactly what they want to write and are able to make a living at it. The vast majority of us, if we feel we must, will work very hard for a long time. We will pour our entire selves into writing for years and years and achieve little or no tangible "success."

So why would you embark on such a journey knowing so few achieve a sense of having arrived? If your answer to this question is that you simply cannot escape the deep desire to write, you may find something of value in my own experience with writing and especially what it has taught me about creative writing.

What is Creative Writing?

I recently experienced a little burst of glee when I learned that some scholars ascribe the original use of the term "creative writing" to Ralph Waldo Emerson. It was Emerson who first infected me with the yearning to write. I remember the moment vividly. I was about twenty years old, lying in the grass, reading *Emerson's Essays*, when suddenly I was overcome by what I can only describe as a kind of rapture. It was not until many years later that I understood the feeling. And it is only with Emerson's own words that I am able to describe it:

"It seemed to me as if I had written the book myself in some former life ... No book before or since was ever so much to me as that ... Cut these words and they would bleed; they are vascular and alive." This is what Emerson said in response to Montaigne's *Essays*. After reading Saint Augustine's *Confessions* he wrote to a friend, "It happens to us once or twice in a lifetime, to be drunk with some book which probably has some extraordinary relative power to intoxicate *us* and none other; and having exhausted that cup of enchantment we go groping in libraries all our years afterwards in the hope of being in Paradise again."

Emerson believed that a single book could decide the course of a person's life. This is the effect *Emerson's Essays* had on me, a young, middle-class, Midwestern girl, far too inexperienced to have anything to say. And yet from that moment on I knew I needed to write. I needed to somehow find my way to a life that would enable me to remain in the company of ideas. All these years later I still feel there is something almost irreverent in my even claiming acquaintance with Emerson's genius. But this is the beauty of Emerson. The very same person who makes us feel we could never do more than cower in his shadow urges us to look inside ourselves for our own spark of genius.

Emerson coined the term "creative writing" in his 1837 "The American Scholar" address to the Phi Beta Kappa Society in Cambridge, Massachusetts. The "scholar" of whom he spoke was much more than a student. He was "Man Thinking." He was "the world's eye, the world's heart." He had learned that "in going down into the secrets of his own mind he descended into the secrets of all minds." And that "the deeper he dives into his privatest, secretest presentiment, to his wonder he finds, the most acceptable, most … universally true."

The person Emerson was speaking of, and to, in "The American Scholar" was a person in love with ideas. A person who opened every book hoping to discover new ones, hoping to be rearranged in a way that would bring about another rush of ideas in his own mind. A person for whom that exhilarating flow of ideas was the very thing that gave life meaning for him. And so he was drawn inescapably to the art of writing. Most important, he was driven by forces entirely "creative" in the purest sense of the word. His urge was to contribute to the ongoing creation and the *forwardness* of life.

This, I believe, is what Emerson meant by "creative writing." He was of course not referring to the literary classification that has emerged in the years since, or what some call "imaginative writing," works of fiction and poetry and plays. What Emerson thought of as creative writing was writing that possesses its own intrinsic value. First, to the writer, through the process of writing it, and then as a contribution to the world of ideas.

When we think of creative writing in this way we see that what matters is not what form our writing takes, or any of the usual measures of what gives writing value. What matters in Emersonian creative writing is the inspiration, the intention, the process, and most of all, the spirit of contribution.

Creative Reading

"First we eat, then we beget, first we read then we write."

The interesting thing about Emerson's coining of the term "creative writing" is that at that point in "The American Scholar" he was talking about reading: "He that would bring home the wealth of the Indies must carry out the wealth of the Indies. There is then, creative reading as well as creative writing."

What Emerson carried out in his own wealth from the Indies was surely as much as a human being can manage in a lifetime. He sought out all of the great thinkers before him from all parts of the world, in literature, philosophy, history, science, the sacred texts of world religions, poetry from East and West. He read Plato in numerous translations and returned to him repeatedly throughout his life. He revered Montaigne and Shakespeare and Goethe, and wrestled with Hume for a number of years. Coleridge, Bacon, Wordsworth and Madame de Stael were also important forces in his life, as was his contemporary, Thomas Carlyle, with whom he corresponded in friendship for many years. The more we learn about Emerson the more the lists of his readings just keep growing. As his brother Charles put it, he was like the "epicure at a long table who would send away no dish untasted."

The idea that we are what we eat — and what we eat *ate* — this is also true of what we take into our minds. What we read becomes part of us. It seeps into our beings and redirects us. It teaches us who we are and what we believe. What we read over our lifetime, even the things we do not entirely recall — they are all part of us. They are embedded in our minds and in our souls. When we read Emerson we are taking in the collective wisdom of all he devoured, all of the thoughts and ideas he embraced as his own and to which he gave new arrangement, new expression.

All those years ago when I fell under Emerson's spell, surely through some other internal apparatus than the mind I was equipped with at the time, I was set on a path of creative reading. From that time on, however unconsciously, I was reading the works that would one day fuel my own writing. In my case this meant I would also be reading *up*.

When we read *up* we gravitate toward books that not only inspire us but challenge us, books in which we may not readily grasp every word, every passage, every idea; we have to spend time with them and read them deeply in order to fully absorb them. This is why it was so invaluable in my young life to be captivated by Emerson. For he also taught me to read the way he did — as Robert Richardson described it in *Emerson: Mind on Fire*, as a "high grader in a gold mine"— carefully sifting through every single nugget, vigilantly watching for those shimmering few, keeping only the finest to take away with me.

If my experience with Emerson strikes a chord in you, perhaps because of a similar experience with another creative writer, you will understand why I said from the start that my thoughts would perhaps be of value to few aspiring writers. You already recognize that you too are a "high grader" in your reading. Simply put, where some people read to become lost in books, you read to become found.

Emerson thought of escapist reading as "a fool's paradise" — an idea I'm convinced he would rub out of his published writings if he could. He read so entirely for inspiration and to fuel his own thinking, he simply could not relate with any other approach to reading. He was also surrounded all his life by people who were equally passionate and purposeful in their reading. Given the opportunity I believe he would tell us to carefully guard against such thinking — that "high graders" are above other kinds of readers. He would say that true creativity requires the opposite kind of feeling. It requires a genuine sense of humility and an absolute openness to powers greater than our own.

What kind of books do "high graders" read? Emerson also provided us with an easy answer to this question. We read creative writing. We read works by authors who might identify themselves by any of many different names — "philosopher," "poet," "fiction-writer," "playwright," "scientist," "historian," "literary critic," or simply, "writer" — but they are all *creative* writers. They are consciously contributing to the world of ideas.

I believe Emerson would tell you that if creative writing is your true calling that, even if you have not yet put down a single word, even if you have no earthly idea what you might one day write, you are already on your path if you are reading. Read everything that speaks to you. And take from what you read every idea you wish to carry with you, every idea you wish to see advanced. You cannot help but do this as long as you are engaged in your own creative reading.

Who is Emerson?

Ralph Waldo Emerson has been called "America's philosopher," "the first philosopher of the American spirit," "the purest of American seers," "the dominant sage of the American imagination." He has been identified as a "literary artist," an "imaginative writer," an "intuitive sage poet," a "popular philosopher" — the list goes on. There has also been a great deal of discussion over the years about which descriptor most aptly applies, as perhaps more than any other writer, Emerson is difficult to reduce to a single one. As George Santayana put it, "he belonged by nature to that mystical company of devout souls that recognize no particular home."

Emerson most often referred to himself as a "scholar." He was a person driven to learning and to the self-expression that makes learning complete. He was his own "American Scholar," a creative reader and creative writer. He devoted his life to the life of the mind. As for the question of whether he was a philosopher or a literary artist, he answered this question in his first published work, *Nature*: "the true philosopher and the true poet are one, and a beauty which is truth, and a truth, which is beauty, is the aim of both."

Emerson was a poet in his soul. He began writing verse in his earliest years as soon as he had learned to write. As a boy he was regularly lifted up by the town grocer and placed on a sugar barrel so he could entertain the locals with his recitations of poetry. Milton, Pope and Campbell were his favorites as a child. "Poet" remained his highest aspiration and an important part of his identity all his life. As it turned out, the written word was indeed his art form. But poetry flows as poetry must. In Emerson's case, into his journals, his lectures, letters, and especially his essays. This is where we find his finest poetry.

In Emerson's day in Puritan New England an intellectual life and a religious life were essentially one and the same. He was an eighth-generation preacher, a role he had been groomed for by the powerful women in his life, especially his father's sister, Mary Moody Emerson, who was the most significant intellectual force among the people in Emerson's life. His father, the minister of the First Church of Boston, died when Waldo was seven years old. His mother and his Aunt Mary saw him through the Harvard Divinity education that had come to be a given among Emerson men. When Emerson left the ministry at the age of twenty-nine he was not only throwing off the enormous weight of his ancestors and all of the pressures of the religious culture in which he lived, he was breaking with the people he loved most in the world. He was leveling a blow that could only be viewed by his family as the worst possible assault against them. This was perhaps the real beginning of Emerson's life as an artist. The kind of artist he implored each of us to be.

A true artist is a seeker after truth. It was the search for truth that drove Emerson. So when he found he could not remain in the church and at the same time pursue an authentic spiritual life, he had no choice but to forge another path and build a meaningful life for himself as the solitary soul he was. He moved on to become an independent scholar, a man of letters, and a major force in our nation's "golden age of oratory." His lectures on the subjects of his choosing he developed into his essays: "Self Reliance," "Nature," "Experience," "The Over-Soul," "Spiritual Laws," "Circles," "Love," "Art," "History," and many others.

Emerson is widely recognized as the founder or leader of Transcendentalism in America, the spiritual/philosophical movement that emerged in New England in the 1820's and brought a fresh, transformative eye to all inherited creeds and conventions. Though he was certainly a central figure in Transcendentalism — as Oliver Wendell Holmes put it, "the movement borrowed its inspiration more from him than from any other source" — this complex, fluid movement has been as challenging to trace with exactness as its roots in European Romanticism, Neo-Platonism and Eastern thought, and as its codes of belief among the many central figures involved. Though Emerson did identify with and give clarity to some of the ideas championed by Transcendentalists, he became known as the movement's leader by virtue of his commitment to those ideas, his association with the other people involved, and especially because of his character, his credibility, and his fame.

What is important about this distinction is that Emerson was the antithesis of a joiner or even a leader of any group. He resisted "Transcendentalist" as part of his identity as he resisted all "ists." Moreover, Transcendentalism was by no means an organized group. It lacked cohesion for the very reason that it was against, and an answer to, institutionalized beliefs, against the adoption of any doctrine as set in stone. Each of the individuals involved had his or her own conception of what it meant to be a Transcendentalist.

The one trait they most shared, as Catherine Albanese points out, was a consciousness that valued that very individuality. This is perhaps where we see Emerson's influence most of all. He was as independent a thinker as his writings represent him to be. It was his independence of mind, and his defense of every individual's independence of mind, that set him apart in the eyes of his fellow Transcendentalists. He was indeed considered a leader among them. A leader among men. (And for the women in his life, *Women in the Nineteenth Century*, including his dear friend Margaret Fuller, a leader among human beings.)

What was it about Emerson that caused everyone who knew him to feel that his entire power rested squarely on his fundamental character? Even his detractors could not help being taken in by the air of "nobility" and "serenity" that surrounded him. He was a man entirely possessed of himself, grounded in himself in a way that inspired respect even in those who completely disagreed with him. When genius is so often accompanied by tortured personalities and enormous human failings, in Emerson it seems to have resided with ease and created an aura of rare integrity. As Lewis Mumford said in *The Golden Day*, "Emerson answered Tolstoy's demand for essential greatness — he had no kinks." No chinks in his armor. It seems that the worst that could be said of him is that the people in his life always wanted more of him, more from him. At the same time, they felt privileged just to be in his orbit.

What Emerson was committed to above all was consciousness. Conscious faith, conscious thought, conscious life. "We walk about in a sleep," he said, "A few moments of our life we truly live." His vow was to live his life "deliberately," as his friend Thoreau would have put it, and to "do nothing for which he had not the whole world for a reason." Emerson's break with the church was no more a renunciation of his faith than it was a rejection of his family. As Robert Richardson said, "If anything, Emerson believed too much, not too little." Religion, to him was not something that could be separated out from a man like his politics or his education. And it was not something that could be instilled in him by any external force. It was the whole of him. It was "the order and soundness of a man." Emerson's mission was to defend each individual's right to a pure, direct, unmediated relationship with God, with the Universe, with Life.

At the time Emerson was declaring his independence from the church and disavowing established church doctrine, a man in a community thirty miles from him was being persecuted and prosecuted for wearing a beard when beards were not in fashion. All of New England was a climate in which, as John Jay Chapman described it, "the conservatism of politics reinforced the conservatism of religion; and as if these two inquisitions were not enough to stifle the soul of man, the conservatism of business self-interest was superimposed." At the time Emerson's independent voice was first being heard, Alex de Tocqueville was writing in *Democracy in America*, "If great writers have not at present existed in America, the reason is very simply the fact that there can be no literary genius without freedom of opinion, and freedom of opinion does not exist in America."

Emerson learned early that his passion for inquiry could not be accommodated by any established system, by any religious canon or educational curriculum that would deny him access to the entire world of ideas. Even as a schoolboy he benefitted most from his extracurricular reading, which far surpassed the depth and breadth of the reading he did for school. At Harvard he was restricted to certain philosophers, while the ones he found most stimulating, most challenging to his own beliefs, were dismissed or frowned upon. When it came to restricting himself to one belief system through which to view the world, he said, "You don't get a candle to see the sunrise." Emerson's reverence was for the sunrise. He hungered to view it through the teachings of all of the world's great spiritual traditions. What he found in the scriptures of India, the wisdom of China, the poetry of Persia, in Buddhism, Zoroastrianism, Islam, were new insights about the nature of God, the role of humanity in the evolving universe, the virtues that are central to all religions, the true moral way for a man to live.

As O. W. Firkins said in his 1915 *Ralph Waldo Emerson*, "Emerson brought into the service of the religious instinct a larger amount and greater variety of material than was ever applied to that function by any other of the sons of men."

When Emerson first came together with some of his friends to explore ideas, the group later dubbed the "Transcendentalists," their one rule, as Transcendentalism scholar Philip F. Gura points out, was that "no man should be admitted whose presence excluded the discussion of any topic." As one observer noted, "the only guest not tolerated was intolerance." This was Emerson's position all his life. What he demonstrated through his life and work is that when we are open to *all* ideas, when we find that our own ideas are only nourished and supported by the free absorption of others — even, or perhaps especially, contrary ones — our expression also takes on an openness. Emerson's writings are not directed to any group or sect. They do not serve any dogma or ideology. Instead, as Randall Fuller said, they "assert the disappointing incompleteness of ideology itself." They speak to all and inspire all to new thought, to new understanding. This is one of the great lessons we find in Emerson. The highest creativity comes to the mind that is open.

Emerson spent his life at the centermost point between religion and philosophy, between spirituality and science, between religion and ethics. He remained firmly rooted in the one place from which he could speak directly from the soul and about the soul. He not only lived every day an examined life, he rethought life itself. And he did so in open view of his listeners and his readers. What he emphasized for all of the creative minds that would follow him is that true creativity is not just about creating but also about recreating. It is about being a "remaker of what man has made."

Emerson's profound influence on other literary luminaries is well known — Thoreau, Whitman and Dickinson, to name a few. I was personally thrilled to uncover some of the not-so-well-known lines that have been drawn — from Emerson to Henri Bergson, for instance, the French philosopher and author of *Creative Evolution,* and to Teilhard de Chardin, whose *Phenomenon of Man* has held the same place of permanence in my life as *Emerson's Essays* — and clearly, to the now obscure Jeanne de Vietinghoff, whose *The Understanding of Good* was one of my greatest personal finds. The fact is that there are endless lines that have been drawn between Emerson and the great thinkers and writers who have fallen under his influence, many of whom have held him in a place of absolute singularity. Olive Schreiner said that Emerson's works were like a bible to her. Margaret Fuller said it was from Emerson that she "first learned what is meant by an inward life." And Maurice Maeterlinck said, "He comes to many at the moment when he ought to come, and at the very instant when they were in mortal need."

Some of the finest literary scholars from Emerson's time to the present have found that it is impossible to overstate Emerson's influence in the literary world. As Joel Porte expressed it, "Emerson provided a new impetus and direction for thought and writing in his time and definitely changed the shape of our literary history." Joel Myerson says, "Every major critical trend in American literary study since 1900 has dealt with Emerson in some fashion. He is here to stay." Harold Bloom even asserts that "From Emerson's moment to ours, American authors either are in his tradition, or else in a counter-tradition originating in opposition to him."

This is another group of Emersonian lines, as bold as any, though unfamiliar to most of us — the lines from Emerson to the literary scholars who know him as well as Emerson can be known. One cannot read the works of these scholars, people who have at their command the entire expanse of literature in the English language, and not be struck by the depth of impact Emerson has had in their lives. Harold Bloom says, "Emerson is with me daily, more frequently even as I age, for I need his highly individual wisdom so that I may survive." And Lawrence Buell's *Emerson*, he says, he began at the age of twenty-six and completed at sixty-two, and "if it persuades others that Emerson is worth pondering for so long a time, I shall be very glad."

But the largest group of Emersonian lines extends to the countless readers and writers whose voices will perhaps never be heard, whose works will never be in print, or if they are will be known to few. And yet these creative readers and writers would tell us that it is impossible to measure the courage and the inspiration they have received from the expression of this single man. They would even tell us that it is because of Emerson's influence that their own creative work is quite enough.

Emerson speaks to the kind of writer who has no choice but to write, the writer for whom "that which is for him to say lies as a load on his heart until it is delivered." For writers who experience this level of yearning, he gives us what we need in order to begin our own writing, in order to see our writing through and make it our own. As Harold Bloom says, "He gives us to ourselves." He assures us that "the only literary and critical method is oneself."

Even more important than the courage Emerson instills in us for our own creative work is what he gives us through his. This is where we find the real divide between those who are deeply inspired by Emerson and those who are simply frustrated by his writing or unmoved by his ideas. As Paul Elmer More explains, "If our dormant intuition answers to his, we are profoundly kindled and confirmed; otherwise his sentences may rattle ineffectually about our ears." Above all, Emerson speaks to the writer for whom his unique brand of idealism reaffirms our own.

In the words of Octavius Frothingham, the first historian of *Transcendentalism in New England*, "For those who need an atmosphere for wings, who require the impulse of great motives, the lift of upbearing aspirations ... for the imaginative, the passionate ... who live in the region of serene ideas ... Emerson is the master."

It was impossible to read Harold Bloom's bold assertion that "every strong American thinker and writer since Emerson has been an Emersonian or an anti-Emersonian" and not call up one of Emerson's own statements: "As thinkers, men have ever divided into two sects, Materialists and Idealists." Emerson made this statement in the opening passage of his 1842 lecture "The Transcendentalist," which he gave only after the descriptor had been publicly foisted upon him by people who had no idea what Transcendentalism was. He described it in a single word: Idealism. "Idealism as it appears in 1842." (If Emerson identified with any "ism," Idealism was one he took full ownership of.) Is it a great leap to draw up this Emersonian delineation, idealists and non-idealists, in relation to writers? The more we know Emerson, the more we think not.

In a world where the vast majority of literature, the vast majority of art, calls our attention to every imaginable human frailty, to every dark corner of human life, Emerson lifts us up. He persuades us as he did Maeterlinck that "life is strange enough, profound enough, great enough, to need no other end than itself." He inspires us to live in and to take sustenance from the life of the mind, and the life of the Universal Mind of which we are all part. He reminds us that our entire material existence is but a fragment of our larger spiritual life. So if we need nourishment, if we need affirmation for our deepest, idealistic instincts, instincts that can be trampled to death in a materialistic world, Emerson gives us everything we need.

Why is Emerson especially important if you are an American aspiring writer? We would be hard pressed to find an American writer, or an American, who has had more influence on the psyche of America, on our religious thought, our political and social thought, on all of the ideas we hold central to "Americanism." As Richard Geldard asserts, "Emersonian thought was not a minor, Romantic trend in religion or philosophy. Rather, it was an evolutionary mutation of the core of American consciousness ... we are who we are as a nation because of it." And as Harold Bloom again emphasizes Emerson's enormous presence in our lives, "The lengthened shadow of our American culture is Emerson's ... The mind of Emerson is the mind of America."

Ralph Waldo Emerson was born less than thirty years after the birth of our nation. The American Revolution began in sight of his grandfather as he peered out an upstairs window of the family home in Concord, the same home where Emerson wrote his first draft of *Nature*. Emerson personally felt every one of our nation's earliest and deepest growing pains, and few Americans have had more extensive knowledge of the period in which they lived. As one of the most important voices of his time he had personal relationships with the other literary figures of his era and engaged directly with key American leaders, including Lincoln, on the subject of slavery. He witnessed the beginnings of American democracy, American government, industry, education, transportation, the national labor union, the displacement of Native Americans, the Mexican War, the Civil War, the settling of the West. He spoke out on and was involved in more national suffering, more rapid growth and sweeping change than Americans of later generations could imagine. He was not only "a great American," as American historian Perry Miller assessed him, "he understood as well as any the magnificent but agonizing experience of what it is to be, or to try to be, an American."

As Lewis Mumford put it, in *The Golden Day*, "the promise of America ... had seeped into every pore of Emerson's mind." He believed in it the way he believed in the boundless resources in the human soul. His appeal to the American scholar, the American poet, was for a new voice, a distinctly American voice, one that would "fill the postponed expectations of the world with something better than the exertions of mechanical skill ... Who can doubt, that poetry will revive and lead in a new age."

> It seems so easy for America to inspire and express the most expansive and humane spirit; new born, free, healthful, strong, the land of the laborer, of the democrat, of the philanthropist, of the believer ... she should speak for the human race. It is the country of the Future.

What Emerson asks us to do, especially as American writers, is to aspire to nothing less than "world making" verse. He believed this was the true calling of the creative writer, to contribute to the making of a better world.

Whenever I think of the Emersonian divide to which Harold Bloom alluded — the one between those who are inspired by Emerson and those who are baffled by his appeal — I now recall a scene Ralph Rusk described in his 1949 biography, *The Life of Ralph Waldo Emerson*. I see Massachusetts congressman and education reformer Horace Mann sitting in rapt attention, listening to Emerson speak, perceiving him as "a man stationed in the sun," a man whose words were "to human life what Newton's Principia was to mathematics." I see Mann and others in the audience completely mesmerized by Emerson. And as Mr. Rusk pointed out, sitting right next to Mann was a man who could only complain of a headache.

Emerson is not for everyone. He is not for every writer. And whether the divide is actually as stark as the split between idealists and non-idealists — this is merely additional food for thought. What is absolutely certain is that if we fall under the influence of Emerson, if we write in the Emersonian tradition, our writing will be filled with hope.

As Stephen Whicher beautifully stated in *Freedom and Fate: An Inner Life of Ralph Waldo Emerson*, "Emerson believed in the dignity of human life more unreservedly, almost, than any one who has ever written. Man possesses, he felt, an unlimited capacity for spiritual growth and is surrounded by influences that perpetually call on him for the best he has of insight and greatness and virtue and love. We think more meanly now, no doubt more truly, of ourselves and our world. But as long as we retain any self-respect, something in us must answer — whatever the second thoughts — to the faith in man that invigorates every page of his volumes. To reject Emerson utterly is to reject mankind."

Ralph Waldo Emerson was a "philosopher" in the purest sense of the word in that he was a "lover of wisdom." He was a philosopher if we see in his ideas as Lewis Mumford did, "a philosophy that resumed the full gamut of human experience it had known in Pythagoras and Plato." Emerson was a "poet" if we believe as he did that the poet is "the world's eye, the world's heart" and that poetry has "nothing less than the creation of man and nature as its end." He was a "mystic," a "sage" if we respond to him as many have, as a "sort of living essence," a "visitant from a higher sphere," a man "who habitually dwelt in that ampler and diviner air to which most of us, if ever, only rise in spurts." Emerson was a "prophet" if we too believe in the unshakable power of wisdom and virtue and courage and hope. And yet, as William James astutely concluded at the centenary celebration of Emerson's life, "If we must define him in one word, we have to call him Artist." To be even more specific, Emerson was a creative writer.

Reading Emerson

"Not every man can read them, but they will reward him who can."
Emerson, on the written works of Emanuel Swedenborg

Emerson's extraordinary literary style has been the subject of endless analysis and criticism among scholars and is the first thing any reader remarks about when speaking of Emerson. One cannot read a page of any one of his essays and not see clearly why this is so. Emerson is not an easy read. He was not easy for his contemporaries and he is certainly not today, not in an American culture that has little time for anything. And this above all is what Emerson requires. He requires time. As Lewis Mumford said, he must be climbed.

As my hope is to persuade you, aspiring writer to aspiring writer, to make the effort to read Emerson, I am going to share what I think is important to know about him to make the climb a little more understandable.

Edward Emerson, in his biography of his father, said that Emerson "stood for a freer thought and expression than American literature had yet known." This is certainly part of Emerson's literary legacy. And yet being an innovator in the field of literature was the furthest thing from Emerson's mind. He was a man obsessed with ideas. His "style" can only be described as "modeling active thinking," or "long inner conversations," or "presenting himself in the act of thinking." He is difficult to read because we are immersed in the thought processes of a brilliant intellect caught in the grip of his own ideas.

One of the most telling things Emerson said about his writing he confided to his journal. He said, "I can no more manage these thoughts that come into my head than thunderbolts." And yet he did manage them. And he managed to present them in forms that would evoke in his readers the same sense of thunderbolts. As John Jay Chapman described it, "he succeeded in delivering himself of his thought with an initial velocity and carrying power such as few men ever attained. He has the force at his command of the thrower of the discus."

Stephen Whicher perhaps better than anyone helps us to see what it was about Emerson that could not help being reflected in his manner of expression. He says, "Thinking, for Emerson, was not a special activity … it was life itself … Because he was distracted by little else he experienced and conveyed the adventure of thought, the daily plunge of the mind into the unknown, with an urgency almost unique in literature. If the function of an artist is to bring something to life for us, to make us see, then Emerson is an artist who makes us see the creative energy of thinking, the original leap and grasp of the mind in action." What we are witnessing in Emerson, he says, is "the action of a superior imagination taking possession of its world."

No analysis of Emerson's writing has any real meaning until we first look at the most extraordinary thing about it, which is its powerful somatic effect. Virginia Woolf described it as "an extraordinary effect of exaltation, as though the disembodied mind were staring at the truth." For those to whom Emerson speaks, he speaks profoundly. He rearranges us in a way that is both life-altering and life-affirming. It is not an intellectual effect. It cannot even be entirely explained as an emotional one. It is an effect that *transcends* both the intellect and the emotions. It happens soul to soul, which was precisely Emerson's aim. The more we learn about Emerson the more we come to appreciate this remarkable power and how it developed within him.

Emerson was trained as a preacher. He had generations of preacher-blood running in his veins. His ear was tuned to the "primitive poetry of the soul," which he found both in scripture and in classical poetry, the cadences of which had surely reverberated in his ears since his recitations of poetry in childhood. He also lived his entire life, almost as much as his friend Thoreau, under the spell of Nature. He walked in the woods daily. And the thoughts he took with him there, the thoughts that emerged there, absorbed some of the rhythms and the music he heard — the music his Aunt Mary called, "the music of the soul." And, as his Aunt Mary surely impressed upon him, the soul makes it own music. It asks only to be transcribed exactly as it comes to us.

Mary Moody Emerson, more than any other person in Emerson's life, influenced his literary style. Her influence began when "Waldo" was a boy and she wrote the family devotions each day that he and his brothers recited aloud. It continued through forty years of rich correspondence, which Emerson valued as much as any in his life. Mary was a fierce intellectual, passionately versed in literature and philosophy, who never hesitated expressing her thoughts exactly as they came to her. Though she was widely known as a deep "eccentric" (the word hardly describes her wild, paradoxical, combustible personality) for Emerson she was his first and strongest real-life exemplar of a ferociously independent mind. Emerson relied on Mary throughout his life, especially for the naysayer role she eagerly played in the evolution of his ideas. He also admired her unique writing style, which he described as "inimitable, unattainable by talent, as if caught from some dream." Clearly, there was one bit of advice she gave him that Emerson fully absorbed — "Sublimity of motive must precede sublimity of style." Though Mary never forgave her nephew for his rejection of her Calvinistic beliefs, she could not help taking pride in the person he became and in the utterly self-governed manner of expression that in many ways reflected hers.

As a preacher in his early years and an orator all his life, Emerson's success in reaching people came from standing in front of groups of people and speaking to them. He was so gifted as an orator that even people who later said they had not understood a single word of his lectures felt they had been in the presence of greatness. Those who did understand them described them as transformative. The young Walt Whitman, then reviewing for a New York newspaper wrote, "It was one of the richest and most beautiful compositions, both for its matter and style, we have ever heard anywhere, at any time." James A. Garfield who later became president of the United States said he dated his real intellectual life from the hour he sat "dazed by the new vision Emerson opened before him." The poet James Russell Lowell said, "There was a tone in it that awakened all elevating associations ... It left you feeling that something beautiful had passed that way, something more beautiful than anything else, like the rising and setting of stars. Every possible criticism might be made of it but one — that it was not noble ... It was as if a creature from some fairer world had lost his way in our fogs, and it was our fault, not his."

Emerson believed that an inspired orator, an orator "inwardly and desperately drunk with conviction," could awaken in his listeners their deepest consciousness and cause them to "enter into universal truth." He believed that an orator's entire power was in the strength of his ideas. One of his models for an inspired orator was Edward Taylor, the famous preacher from the Boston Seamen's Bethel who is also thought to have been Melville's model for Father Mapple in *Moby Dick*. When we read what Emerson wrote in his journal after hearing Taylor speak, we cannot help seeing the striking similarity to people's reactions to Emerson's orations — as well as to the written works those orations became. "The utter want and loss of all method, the ridicule of all method, the bright chaos come again of his bewildering oratory, certainly bereaves it of power, — but what splendor! what sweetness! what richness! what depth! what cheer! How he conciliates, how he humanizes! how he exhilarates and ennobles!"

"The utter want and loss of all method, the ridicule of method" — these words can be found in every possible variation in the criticism that has followed Emerson from his day to the present. For people to whom Emerson does not speak, or who have perhaps not given him the time he demands, his essays can seem terribly disjointed, lacking in unity and logical structure. Even those to whom he does speak can suffer the impression, as Barbara Packer put it, "of sentences that lie on the page like steel filings when no magnet is present." Theodore Parker, Emerson's fellow Transcendentalist, described his sentences as, "an army all officers — but they are advancing on a long march," he added. James Russell Lowell described Emerson's writings as "a chaos filled with shooting stars."

As Paul Elmer More explains, where Emerson's essays "fail to reach the reader's heart, it is not because they are fundamentally disjointed, as if made up of sentences jostled together like so many mutually repellent particles; but because from the manner of his composition

Emerson often missed what he might have learned from Plato's *Phaedrus* was the essence of good rhetoric ... the consciousness of his hearer's mind as well as of his own."

Was Emerson unconscious of the hearer's mind? Of the challenges readers would face in his seemingly disjointed presentation of his thoughts? Clearly, he was plagued by these very concerns when he sent off his essays to Carlyle and confessed to his friend that they seemed to him "only boards and logs tied together." And when he wrote in his journal, "If Minerva offered me a gift and an option, I would say give me continuity." And yet if we look at these expressions of doubt in Emerson as at all indicative of what he actually achieved, we will be only grazing the surface of Emerson. We will be missing the enormous genius that he most of all did not recognize.

Emerson had no choice but to write the way he did, just as he had no choice but to write. This is why in the end he published his essays just as they had come to him, just as they remained on the pages no matter how much he may have wanted to rework them into forms less challenging to his readers. On some level he knew they had assumed their particular forms by some power of their own; they could no more be reworked into other forms than a sprig of honeysuckle can be made into a maple leaf. They had met his own test for what makes true poetry — that it is filled with ideas "so passionate and alive that like the spirit of a plant or an animal it has an architecture of its own and adorns nature with a new thing."

Does it underestimate Emerson's literary prowess to say he did not deliberately write the way he did, that he had no choice? On the contrary. It only emphasizes that for Emerson, his prized "organic form" was something that came to him instinctively, unavoidably, maybe even unconsciously. Yes, he could have discussed literary theory in boundless depth with Bacon and Goethe and Coleridge. He did discuss aesthetic theory with many of his time. But when he closed the door of his study and buried himself in his work, there was no room in his brain for thoughts of form. His own authentic expression filled the whole of him.

One of the fascinating things about Emerson's writing (and perhaps about true literary criticism) is that the most incisive criticism of it only takes us deeper into Emerson's genius. Paul Elmer More's choice of words, for instance, "like so many mutually repellent particles" (from Emerson's own expression) is a perfect example. It leads us into an understanding of how Emerson's style actually reflected his ideas.

Emerson's commitment to the independence of each individual's mind was central to everything he wrote. His aim was to provoke thought and to lead the reader to his own ideas. He routinely juxtaposed two antithetical ideas, two "mutually repellent particles," and made the argument for each, inviting the reader into deeper thought. As his son Edward said, both the devout Christian and the agnostic could have found in his father's works "endless ammunition for their opposition to the other." And yet Emerson did not claim to have the answer for either of them. As Lawrence Buell said, "He insists that even though he may feel in the grip of Truth, what he has to say is nothing more than glimpses or fragments, which his listeners must complete."

> He in whom the love of Truth predominates will keep himself aloof from all moorings, and afloat. He will abstain from dogmatism, and recognize all the opposite negations between which, as walls, his being is swung.

From the time Emerson became enchanted with Socrates as a young man and all throughout his life he learned from Plato that the only authentic relationship with truth was one of constant "unknowing." He learned that only a steady flow of a dialectic of opposites could bring one into contact with glimpses of truth. And glimpses of truth were all that were possible, even for the most devoted seeker. Emerson believed that truth was in a constant state of becoming and that "the truest state of mind, rested in, becomes false." He viewed "every moment of the existence of the universe as a new creation" and part of the ongoing creation of life. His manner of expression, his style of writing, was every bit a testament to his beliefs.

If we are looking for someone to tell us in a straightforward manner, "This is truth. This is what to believe" — we will not find this in Emerson. We will not find this in any artist. An artist embeds his truths in his art and offers his art to the world. He says, "Take what you will from it, whatever it is that you see." What we see in Emerson's art, what we experience because of it, he hopes will lead us to our own truths. He insists that what gives value to any idea, to any belief, is our recognition of it as our own.

One of the more interesting things I have discovered in my own exploration of Emerson is that the deeper we delve, into him, and into the criticism of him, the more the former cancels out the latter. The more we become satisfied that all reproach of him has been nullified — and by his own eloquent expression.

One common attack on Emerson, for instance, has been for his inconsistencies and contradictions. And yet as we explore Emerson's own thoughts on inconsistency and contradiction, we come to recognize one of Emerson's greatest strengths. As Ralph Rusk said, it was precisely Emerson's level of comfort with inconsistency and contradiction that made his mind so "conspicuously valuable."

> I know of no more irreconcilable persons ever brought to annoy and confound each other ... than are sometimes actually lodged by nature in one man's skin.

> Speak what you think today in words as hard as cannon balls, and tomorrow speak what tomorrow thinks in hard words again, though it contradict every thing you said today.

> What is a man born for but to be a Reformer, a Re-maker of what man has made ... imitating that great Nature ... which sleeps no moment on an old past ... yielding us every morning a new day, and with every pulsation a new life?

> So I will forget my yesterdays and hear only the sweet bells of today.

And of course his most well known statement — "A foolish consistency is the hobgoblin of little minds."

As Evelyn Barish explains in *Ralph Waldo Emerson: Roots of Prophesy,* Emerson had learned through the struggles of his own life "not to deny uncertainty, but to gather the moral strength to live with it." Doubt, to Emerson, as his friend James Cabot observed, "was not the end of wisdom, it was the means." Stephen Whicher even insists that Emerson's power rested on this very thing — "on the compulsions and conflicts, the revelations and the doubts, the glories and the fears which struck fire in his imagination." And Jay William Hudson, after plumbing the depths of Emerson's beliefs, held him up as "the champion of the royal virtue of honest inconsistency." In other words, the inconsistencies, the uncertainties and the contradictions are not in Emerson. As Emerson continually reminded us, they are in life.

This is just one example of the criticisms of Emerson that have been laid to rest for me by Emerson himself. And not out of any response to criticism. Emerson did not defend his ideas. He presented no arguments that needed defending. No systems of thought. No systems of belief. As Cabot said, "He was only noting single aspects of truth as they struck him, trusting that every one would do the like for himself." And as Virginia Woolf followed, he simply had "the poet's gift of turning far, abstract thoughts ... into something firm and glittering."

Emerson wrote as he read, as the "high-grader in the gold mine," emerging from the mine as passionate about sharing his finds as he was about unearthing them. He also wrote as he spoke, "inwardly and desperately drunk with conviction." He had learned well from his teachers, both the ones he found in books and the ones he knew in life, that the speaker, the writer, is only as powerful as his own belief in the ideas he shares.

As John Jay Chapman said in his brilliant 1898 essay, "Emerson," "Emerson consistently and utterly expressed himself ... never troubling himself for a moment with what literature was or how literature should be created." He was unflinchingly faithful to his own conviction that "if a man would be anything, he must be himself."

Paul Elmer More, the same scholar who perfectly described every reader's experience with Emerson, of "sentences jostled together like so many mutually repellent particles," also described what Emerson achieved through his writings — in the world of literature, in the world of thought: "As a steady force in the transmutation of life into ideas and as an authority in the direction of life itself, he has obtained a recognition such as no other of his countrymen can claim ... He stands for something that the world is not likely to let die."

Yes, Emerson is a challenging read. His style of writing alone has inspired exhaustive scholarship. And though it is fascinating to think that one man's writing could have stirred such in-depth analysis, for me, the keenest analysis has come from the scholars with the longest lenses. F.O. Matthiessen, in his study of the *American Renaissance* said that the best way to understand Emerson's style is to "remember where he always threw his last emphasis." Emerson's last emphasis, always, was on the life of the soul. It was on ideas that can awaken souls. His works can only be truly absorbed when we read them as he intended, as free of thoughts of style and form as he was when he wrote them.

In reading *Emerson's Essays*, it helps to remember that what we are reading was originally presented as an oration before an audience. It helps to even imagine ourselves among one of those audiences, which were consistently described as spellbound. As Horace Mann described the experience, "It was almost impossible to catch the great beauty and proportion of one truth before another was presented ... It was one of the most splendid manifestations of a truth-seeking and truth-developing mind I ever heard." If we imagine Emerson in front of us, speaking the words we are reading, we not only experience a man standing in the midst of a torrent of ideas, we hear his own response to each of them. We hear that he is as enraptured by ideas as a person can be.

Reading Emerson, we have the opportunity to spend time with those ideas, to reflect on them in ways Emerson's audiences could not. We are able to go back and review passages that in the spoken word could only have struck his listeners as the "thunderbolts" they described. Thunderbolts we are able to examine close-up and return to again and again for the deeper understanding we find each time. We are able to reread difficult, convoluted passages that seem to go on forever without ever meeting up with an earlier thought. And then to discover in that very passage an idea that takes our breath away.

It is having our breath taken away by ideas that brings readers back again and again to Emerson. And the ideas he brings to life, the inspiration he brings — for the aspiring creative writer — this is perhaps his greatest legacy. For as he said, the highest effect of art is "to make new artists."

Self-Reliance

"I will not live out of me
I will not see with others' eyes."

"Self-Reliance" is Emerson's defining essay and the foundation upon which his entire legacy stands. For the aspiring creative writer, it is perhaps the most important piece of writing you will read. If you do not yet know this essay you will do yourself an immense favor to purchase your own copy and read it as slowly and as carefully as you have ever read anything. For what you will find in this single essay is the best advice you will find for how to go about your writing.

True creative writing *is* self-reliance. It is self-reliance in one of its purest, most active forms. There is no act that calls upon us more to be ourselves, to rely on ourselves, and to dig deeply within ourselves to discover and to own our own truths.

Emerson would be happy to have you read "Self-Reliance" knowing as little of him as he knew of Plato. As Ralph Rusk said, few have absorbed Plato's spirit as completely as Emerson. And he did so without any knowledge of Plato or Plato's life, only of his ideas. This is the way I experienced Emerson for years. And yet learning about Emerson's life and how he came into his own self-reliance has deepened my appreciation for this powerful essay. It has convinced me even more that "Self-Reliance" is essential reading for every creative writer.

If ever a person were born into a predestined identity, an identity defined by his family's traditions and his family's values, it was Emerson. He was marked early on, by his own ambition as well as his family's, as heir apparent to the Emerson pulpit. Like every other human being he had to find his own way to a life that was his own. For Emerson this meant struggling against a mighty tide. And who was the first person to influence his emergence as a self-reliant individual? Ironically, it was the one who most wanted to set his course for him.

Mary Moody Emerson was the driving force in the education of the Emerson children. As Emerson described it, she imposed such "immeasurably high standards which nothing else in education could supply." From the time her nephews were young boys Mary guided their reading and held them to account for their individual thoughts on each text they read. She trained them in reasoning and expression and stimulated them to rigorous discussion. Above all she taught them to rely on their own judgment, to value above all other influences their own independent thought.

From the time his father died and until he came into his own income as an adult, Emerson's family was poor. He spent much of his youth in a basement room in his mother's boarding house where his only view was that of gravestones and abandoned furniture in the neighboring graveyard. He and his four brothers often went hungry and he and William had to share an overcoat in winter and were teased at school about whose turn it was to have a coat today. "Aunt Mary" would sing hymns with the boys when they were hungry and even persuaded them that there was something virtuous in poverty. She especially encouraged them to develop their own inner lives, their own private space in which their thoughts and dreams could sustain them. It was Mary's example and encouragement that started Emerson on the path to a strong inner life.

Perhaps the greatest gift Mary gave her nephew was the courage to be a radical thinker. To stand by his own thought without regard for either the approval or the dissent of others. She also made him comfortable with the uncertainties and the contradictions that must be embraced by every honest seeker of truth. Mary Moody Emerson was a walking-breathing contradiction. She was immovably rooted in pious Calvinism at the same time she was a passionate seeker of spiritual wisdom. She probed and penetrated and questioned all systems of thought — except the one into which she was born. Where she and her nephew finally parted ways was in Emerson's inability to compartmentalize. He recognized no text, no scripture or religious canon as above the same scrutiny he had learned to apply to every text he read.

When "Waldo" entered Harvard at the age of fourteen (not uncommon in those days), he already had an inner life that was far more important to him than anything he found at college. There, he was known as a "mediocre student." As Robert Richardson put it, "he did not shine in the things that Harvard then knew how to measure." Emerson would say that no educational institution, then or now, is committed to true education, which to him meant "the drawing out of the soul." For him this happened not through instruction in Latin and Greek and mathematics but through his own voracious reading, his deep, philosophical correspondence with his Aunt Mary, and above all, his journal, which he began at the age of sixteen under the title "The Wide World."

As Lawrence Buell explains, Emerson used the term "scholar" in a "disruptively anti-professional sense: to commend independent-minded thinking that makes knowledge subserve thought rather than vice versa." Emerson saw little relationship between formal education and true scholarship, the kind of scholarship that "sets genius free." He believed that "education aims to sink what is individual or personal in us," when its real objective should be "to teach self-trust," to recognize a child's true nature and "arm it with knowledge in the very direction in which it points." To Emerson, a scholar was a person awakened to his own critical thought.

On some level Emerson knew early on that he did not belong in the ministry. He even lost his eyesight within weeks of entering Divinity School and did not recover it until he had spent many months reassessing his direction. He accepted his first minister's post determined to remain true to his own conscience. This is where he was up against the mightiest tide of all. As his biographer Gay Wilson Allen described it, "Here was a young man who demanded that the preacher examine everything he said and say nothing he did not honestly, even passionately, believe in, and say it not according to tradition, in well-worn patterns of rhetoric and intonation, but in his own way … Sooner or later this young man with a mind of his own would lose patience with every inherited creed, ritual, and ecclesiastical hierarchy, and demand such complete honesty in every word and deed that no religious institution could satisfy him — or maybe even tolerate him."

Emerson came to disavow conformity of every kind, in religion, in education, in one's entire life. "We do not make a world of our own," he said, "but fall into institutions already made." He believed that when we give ourselves over to prescribed sets of beliefs, this very surrender to powers outside our own beings "scatters our force" and "blurs our character." It makes our beliefs, our ideas, our actions, inauthentic. He believed that "the whole of our social structure — State, School, Religion, Marriage, Trade, Science — has been cut off from its root in the soul, and has only a superficial life." What he demanded for himself and advocated for each human being was absolute liberty to follow one's own intuitive convictions, the convictions one finds in the depths of one's soul.

By the time Emerson gave his Harvard Divinity School Address at the age of thirty-two, he was unable to be anything but forthright about his beliefs. He was then a former minister and the author of *Nature*, invited by the graduating students, not by the faculty. He told the assembly that churches were lifeless and dying because they clung to tradition rather than awakening souls and inspiring virtue. He reproached ministers whose sermons promoted fear rather than love. He asserted his belief that "the faith that stands on authority is not faith," and that "faith makes us, not we it, and faith makes its own forms." He urged the young, aspiring clergy to rise above the "soul-destroying slavery to habit" and to trust in and speak from their own souls.

What Emerson said of his Aunt Mary, that "religion was her occupation," could not have been truer of Emerson himself — even though as he famously stated he found that "in order to be a good minister it was necessary to leave the ministry." As his friend James Cabot said, "Emerson left the pulpit for the lecturer's desk, because he wished to be entirely free to declare the faith that was in him." Religion, to Emerson, was about the individual, lived experience of faith and about centering one's entire life on that inner spiritual life, the life of the soul.

What Emerson took as his ultimate occupation was in fact something much larger than religion, even as he understood it. He aspired to nothing less than restoring the soul to its rightful place — in religion, in philosophy, in education, in the individual consciousness he sought to inspire. As John Jay Chapman put it, "It is as if a man had been withdrawn from the earth and dedicated to condensing and embodying this eternal idea — the value of the individual soul — so vividly, so vitally ... he stands alone in the history of teachers."

Emerson's "Self-Reliance," in fact, may have been more aptly named "Soul-Reliance," this is how strongly Emerson believed in the soul as the essence of self. He believed that within each soul is a deep intuition, a "seeing eye," which perceives truth directly. In its most seeing moments, it beholds universal wisdom and truth. When we are engaged in true self-reliance, this is what we are relying on, this inner sight, which not only puts us in touch with truth, it engages us in a proper relationship with truth, including, as George Kateb described it, "the readiness to treat with sympathetic understanding ideas and values that have no sympathy for one another." It was this benefit of self-reliance, the reliance on his own soul, which brought about the openness to truth that was so characteristic of Emerson.

"Self-Reliance" can of course be simply understood as a rejection of conformity, as a throwing off of "all false ties" and "beginning afresh in one's own consciousness." It can be understood as self-possession, self-trust, self-governance, self-determination. For Emerson, it was all of these things and more. It was the key to an awakened life, a moral life, a meaningful life. It was the most reliable path for an individual to take toward a conscious reuniting with his own soul.

> The one thing in the world, of value, is the active soul. This every man is entitled to; this every man contains within him, although, in almost all men, obstructed,

and as yet unborn. The soul active sees absolute truth; and utters truth, or creates. In this action, it is genius; not the privilege of here and there a favorite, but the sound estate of every man.

Emersonian self-reliance has of course been rejected by many. First, when it is misunderstood as self-centeredness or narcissism, or the hubris of believing that one can have personal insight to universal truths. And secondly, when it is thought of as anti-religious or as advocating reliance on self rather than on God. Of all possible misunderstandings of Emerson, this one is the most ironic, for Emerson was as faith*ful* as any saint or mystic. For him, self-reliance *was* reliance on God. The power he believed resided in the soul was both God-given and the strongest human connection with God. As George Kateb put it in his definitive *Emerson and Self Reliance*, "Emerson's ultimate meaning of self-reliance is to be properly religious." People who object to Emerson's philosophy on religious grounds do so for the same reason his Aunt Mary did, because it does not promote their particular religion.

Is it possible to be a nonbeliever and practice Emersonian self-reliance? Emerson would likely say that the nonbeliever may be more given to the courage it takes to practice true self-reliance, as the nonbeliever has already learned to rely on his own truths in a world that wants to define his truths for him. Though Emerson was steeped in Christianity, one of the steadiest spiritual influences in his life came from men who lived hundreds of years before Christ, Socrates and Plato. For Socrates, the "soul" was the seat of an individual's capacity for intelligence and character. It was his conscience and his moral compass. One can give to "soul" no religious connotation at all and still relate deeply with Emersonian self-reliance.

Obviously there are no two words that can be more easily mischaracterized as self-centeredness or egotism than "self-reliance." And yet this too is an ironic interpretation of Emerson. As Wesley Mott stressed, "For Emerson, genuine individualism was not narcissism or monomania ... it was an answer to these diseases of the self." Emerson's "self-reliance" stands in stark opposition to any philosophy that would be used to justify any self-interest. "The soul stipulates for no private good," he said. "The soul knows no persons." Emerson's devotion to a strong inner life was grounded in his belief that, as Lawrence Buell put it, "the more inward you go, the less individuated you get."

> In listening more intently to our own reason ["reason" to Emerson was the soul's deep intuition], we are not becoming in the ordinary sense more selfish, but are departing more from what is small, and falling back on truth itself and on God.

> A trust in yourself is the height not of pride, but of piety, an unwillingness to learn of any but God himself. It will come only to one who feels that he is nothing.

To some of Emerson's contemporaries of course, "self-reliance" could only be viewed as blasphemy — or at the very least a convenient avoidance of the discipline involved in true religion. What they did not understand, as Stephen Whicher explains, is that "Emerson's 'live from within' was not a means of carefree liberation, but of strenuous and radical self renewal." It was an arduous, self-imposed, painstaking effort at the most challenging discipline of all — consciousness. As Emerson said, "If anyone imagines that this law is lax, let him keep its commandment one day."

Emerson's Essays, especially his "Self-Reliance" caused quite a stir in nineteenth century New England. "It would overturn society and resolve the world into chaos!" one reviewer said, "What a bedlam of egoists would be turned loose on the world if this indiscriminate self-reliance was generally adopted as the sole regulating principle of life." As it turned out, Harriet Martineau's review was perhaps the most prophetic. She predicted for Emerson's essays a thousand years of life.

When I was overcome by the desire to write this book, a book about creative writing, one of the first things I did was to return to Emerson's "Self-Reliance," the work I have revisited more times throughout my life than any other written work. I had no idea of the process that would ensue, or that it would be guided throughout by the same force that had drawn me to writing in the first place.

Why is Emerson's "Self-Reliance" so essential for the aspiring creative writer? This is not something that can be explained in words or ideas or teachings. It is not even something that can be absorbed all at once. For most of us it happens over a lifetime. As Harold Bloom says, "He gives us to ourselves." He reaches into the deepest part of us and lights a flame that once lit can never be extinguished. It is there to light our way to "the one thing in the world of value" — our own "active soul."

I have deliberately quoted sparingly here from "Self-Reliance" as I did not want to deprive you of any bit of the experience of reading it through in its entirety, either for the first time or with your own creative writing in mind. When you do you will be reading an essay that has been examined perhaps as much as any essay ever written. And yet as Emerson would assure you, what you will bring to it will be something brand new.

If you approach this challenging bit of reading as a "high-grader in a gold mine," searching for the gleaming nuggets you might take away with you, you will need only to be a patient miner. You may also find as many have that you experience some inexplicable overall effect, just from having been in the mine. This, even as much as the gleaming nuggets, is what draws readers back to it again and again.

As I reread "Self-Reliance" this time, I realized there was something else about Emerson that was important to share with any aspiring writer who might be reading this powerful essay for the first time.

Emerson was at times provocative. This was part of his passion for ideas and his natural manner of expression. He sometimes said things that taken out of context, or even in context without an understanding of Emerson, can give a mistaken impression of his meaning as well as of him. His rail on philanthropy in "Self-Reliance" is a frightful example. One might think he was a heartless snob. He makes no secret of his genuine irritation with falsely motivated do-gooders. His point is that even charity, in order to be authentic, must come from within. It must be motivated by one's own beliefs and inclinations, not by appearances or outside pressures.

The "Sage of Concord" was anything but heartless. His heart was as deeply educated as his mind. After losing his father at the age of seven and his only sister at eleven, his first passionate love, his wife Ellen, died after only seventeen months of marriage. The second great passion in his life, his first son Waldo, died suddenly at age five. And by all accounts Emerson was never quite the same again. He also buried two of his brothers, Charles and Edward, with whom he was extremely close, and Henry Thoreau and Margaret Fuller, two of his most cherished friends. Emerson was the one in his family to whom every one turned for any kind of help. From the age of fifteen he had promised himself his mother would never be in want, a promise he kept. His mother lived with him and his family until the day she died. (Though his mother has been overshadowed by the larger-than-life sister of her husband, Mary Moody Emerson, Ruth Haskins Emerson was an equally powerful force in Emerson's life. His own assessment of her influence was perhaps expressed best in his assertion that "Men are what their mother's make them.") He also financially supported his brothers and several friends for years and helped care for his younger brother Bulkeley who was cognitively impaired and a lifelong dependent. Emerson was married to his second wife Lydia for forty-six years and had three other children who loved and admired him and felt loved by him. He was looked to for wisdom and counsel by family, neighbors and friends all his life. No one lacking in heart could be perceived by so many as an exemplary human being. Perhaps Emerson's greatest failing was the one his friend Carlyle put his finger on when he said, "Ah! dear Emerson! He thinks that every body in the world is as good as himself."

This time, as I reread "Self-Reliance" with creative writing in mind, the thought also came to me that for those of us who yearn to create it is perhaps as important to contemplate what self-reliance is *not* as it is to understand what it is. Self-reliance has nothing to do with individual identity, with defining or distinguishing ourselves through our creative work. As David Robinson said in *The Spiritual Emerson*, Emersonian self-reliance "has more to do with self-surrender than self-enlargement." It is a "critical self-awareness and a self-confidence shaped by an underlying humility."

Creativity, of course, cannot happen without ego, any more than it can happen without intelligence. Our intelligence and our ego both have important roles in the drive to create and in the creative process. But real creativity, as Emerson understood it, has nothing to do with us.

Creativity, originality — these are things we all sometimes confuse with being different, or radical, or producing something that will set us apart. This is about ego. It is about elevating our own sense of identity. What Emerson taught was that self-reliance is not about standing out from the crowd. It is about drawing our own power from within. As Richard Geldard said in *The Spiritual Teachings of Emerson*, "there is no integrity in rebellion, per se" — not for its own sake. Emerson's writings have not lasted because they were radical. They have lasted because they were filled with truths and because those truths were not tied to any personal source, they belong to all of us. True self-reliance is reliance on something much larger than any one of us.

The Gleam of Light

"A man should learn to detect and watch that gleam of light which flashes across his mind from within."

When I first read these words as a young woman I understood what Emerson meant by them. It was not that I could explain "the gleam of light" in any other words, even to myself. Emerson's words were enough. I knew he was talking about something I had experienced, something I had never before had affirmed as real. Emerson made me trust it. The gleam of light. I remembered those words all my life.

Reading Emerson was one of my first experiences with inspiration. Inspiration is what Emerson looked for in every book he read. It is what fills the pages of every one of his writings. He was as given to inspiration as any writer before him, any writer since.

If Emerson was right, inspiration comes not just from our soul but through our soul from a higher source. The source he called "The Over Soul," the soul "within which every man's particular being is contained and made one with all other." This is what Emerson's reverence for the soul was about — the "Universal Soul," the soul at the centre "for which all things exist, and that by which they are." True inspiration, as Emerson understood it, comes from this higher source. As Vivian Hopkins explained it in

Spires of Form, "Emerson asserts that the artist ... attains direct contact with the Divine Mind, deriving his intuition for creation from a single illuminated moment."

The idea of a "Divine Mind" or "Universal Soul" has been with us a long time. Emerson's "Over Soul" in fact is from a translation of the Sanskrit "At-Man," "the supreme and universal soul," which has been called many different names in many different traditions. Plotinus, the follower of Plato whom some regard as "the mystic Plato," was especially committed to this idea. Plotinus believed that each soul is part of the "Eternal One" and that throughout our earthly lives our souls are yearning to be reunited with the Universal Soul. He believed that the only way to achieve this union was by going *within*. Plotinus was never out of arm's reach of Emerson. He was as steady a force in his life as Plato.

Emerson too believed of the soul that "we belong to it, not it to us." He believed that by following our soul's deep intuition we can come into alignment with the Mind behind all minds, "the Artist back of all artists." "All things are known to the soul," he said. The great writers have found there "all of the wisdom of humanity."

Inspiration is not something any of us can make happen. It is something that happens to us, in its own way, its own time. There are ways we can make ourselves receptive, however. There are things we can do to create an environment within us and around us in which those "gleams of light" can find their way through.

The first, of course, is to keep ourselves in the company of ideas. This is one of the ways Emerson invited inspiration. He spent much of his life taking in the ideas of the inspired thinkers and writers before him. And he never lost sight of his great debt to his forerunners. "We all depend at last on the few heads ... nearest the stars," he said. "Get books that will open your eyes and your ears and ... turn you inside out and outside in ... Take thankfully and heartily all they can give. Exhaust them, wrestle with them, let them not go until their blessings be won."

And yet Emerson also cautioned that though our ideas may be nourished and encouraged by the ideas of others there comes a time when we must put away the books and really listen to our own thoughts. "Great works of art have no more affecting lesson for us than this," he said, "no kernel of nourishing corn can come to him but through his toil bestowed on that plot of ground which is given to him to till." Turning inward and remaining inward for extended periods — this is the most essential prerequisite for any receptivity to true inspiration. Solitude is the only plot of ground from which we can grow anything of our own.

Solitude is becoming an endangered value in our increasingly networked world. We are not only losing touch with personal communication, we are spending less time alone. And yet scientists now tell us that what is going on in our brains when we are in our most quiet, restful state of mind consumes twenty times as much energy as the active life of the mind. Spending time alone is an important thing! And real solitude, the solitude it takes to make room in our brains for "illumination" — this is more than time away from others. It is more than time away from computers and books. It is the time we spend quietly, deliberately, attentively *alone*.

Emerson believed that the best way to be truly alone is to be alone within the depths of Nature. He believed that our inner voice and the voice of Nature are one. As his son Edward observed, "The woods were his best study ... Even in winter storms ... he liked to walk alone at night for the inspiration he ever found in the stars ... There he felt that he saw things healthily, largely, in their just order and perspective ... his eyes saw nothing but instances of ... ever-renewed creative force ... in all things."

> We lie in the lap of immense intelligence, which makes us organs of its activity and receivers of its truth ... Place yourself in the middle of the stream of power and wisdom which flows into you as life, place yourself in the full centre of that flood, then you are without effort impelled to truth.

Jonathan Bishop, in *Emerson on the Soul*, explains that Emerson's "sympathetic identification" with every aspect of Nature evoked in him a "renewed consciousness of himself as a being alive within an organic scene." In Nature, he says, Emerson experienced himself not separate from Nature but one with it, "merged with the totality of all that is."

> The world is ... of one will, of one mind; and that one mind is everywhere active, in each ray of the star, in each wavelet of the pool ... All things proceed out of the same spirit, and all things conspire with it.

Of all the sources of inspiration Emerson spoke of as belonging to all of us, this is the one of which I am most in awe. The truth is I am barely able to relate with it — the power Nature had in Emerson's life. I believe few of us are able to truly relate. Thoreau of course did, because he had the same deep relationship with Nature. And that is what it was for these two men, a profound relationship, one that I believe few human beings experience. And not just because it requires so much time, communing with Nature and learning from Nature and appreciating Nature, but because what these two men brought to that relationship was something rare. I believe that in naming his first book *Nature*, Emerson named his primary source of inspiration.

Fortunately, there was another source of inspiration in Emerson's life with which we are all able to relate: "*My friends*," he said, "the Great God gave them to me."

> High thanks I owe to you ... who carry out the world for me to new and noble depths, and enlarge the meaning of all my thoughts.

Henry Thoreau, Bronson Alcott and Margaret Fuller were among the friends who inspired Emerson. They inspired one another. They would sometimes combine their walks in the woods with their visits with one another and would talk about the books they were reading and process their ideas together. Emerson was deeply nourished by a number of important relationships in his life. His years of correspondence with his Aunt Mary and with Thomas Carlyle were certainly among them.

This is the single thing I have valued most as a writer, the people in my life who have been my highest inspiration. Without true friends, friends I could call on at any time, I would not have had the constitution for all of the alone time that has made such a difference in my life, as a writer and as a human being. As Emerson said, it is one of the purposes of friendship to equip us for solitude. But the most valuable thing that comes from our friends is what happens in conversation with them. We are able to talk with them in a way that is thoroughly liberating. It not only frees us to embrace their ideas, the ideas they offer us as gifts, it brings our own ideas into focus for us as nothing else can. Emerson referred to conversations with friends as "a series of intoxications," and "the true school of philosophy." "We must be warmed by the fire of sympathy," he said, "and be brought into the right conditions and angles of vision." There is nothing more important for creative writers to invest in, he would tell us, than strong, enduring relationships.

And there is another source of inspiration that Emerson would say is invaluable to the creative writer. He would no doubt call it *life*. "No man believes any more than he has experienced," he said. "The scholar loses no hour which the man lives." Emerson would urge us to live full, rich lives and to experience every moment of them as consciously as we can. For every bit of lived experience, he insists, is "convertible into jewels."

> Life is our dictionary ... It is the raw material out of which the intellect moulds her splendid products ... Drudgery, calamity, exasperation, want, are instructors in eloquence and wisdom ...

> The gardener saves every slip, and seed, and peach-stone ... Not less does the writer attend his affairs ... His needs, appetites, talents, affections, accomplishments, are keys that open to him the beautiful museum of human life.

And of course there is a special reason for living a full life — in work, in travel, in everything we do to reach out and beyond our familiar society — and that is the people we meet along the way. The seemingly chance encounters, the fleeting relationships, which can sometimes offer up profound illuminations.

One such experience happened for Emerson when he was a young man on a voyage from Boston to South Carolina and eventually to Florida. It was a health-driven voyage, a much needed respite from both the northern climate and his impending decision about the ministry. Interestingly, the man he met during this trip, Achille Murat, a nephew of Napoleon, with whom he engaged in intense conversation for days aboard ship, was his first exposure to a real-life atheist. Murat's ideas and the intelligence with which he presented them had a powerful impact on Emerson. He was also moved by the depth of mutual respect they achieved. Their time together persuaded Emerson of the "indestructible" nature of his own faith. It also gave him new insight about his direction, something for which he remained grateful to Murat all his life — though they corresponded only once. It is these kinds of stirring encounters with other human beings that give purpose to our living full lives.

More than anything else, I believe Emerson was so receptive to inspiration because of his great hunger for it. He made himself consciously open to it from the time he was a boy. He insisted that we can all make ourselves open to inspiration and receive it in its highest forms. He even believed that those "gleams of light" are always searching our souls for an "unobstructed channel."

Inspiration, some would say, is the first step in every creative process. It is that single moment of illumination that begins the process and propels it on its course. This kind of inspiration can take many different forms. It is different for each of us each time it occurs. It may come in the form of an idea that suddenly flashes across our mind, or a seedling of an idea that grows over time in our mind. It may appear gradually, piece by piece over a number of years until one day we are struck by it as a complete idea. It may even take the form of two ideas seeming to collide, creating a sudden burst of awareness of an inherent connection between the two. Though inspiration is not always something we recognize intellectually in the moment it occurs, it invariably creates a feeling in us that is unlike anything else.

One of my more riveting moments with Emerson was when I came upon an entry in his journal where he described the experience of a sudden flash of inspiration. He described its effect on him the moment it came rushing through him:

> The joy which will not let me sit in my chair, which brings me bolt upright to my feet, and sends me striding around my room like a tiger in his cage, and I cannot have composure and concentration enough even to set down in English words for the thought which thrills me — is not that joy the certificate of the elevation? What if I never write a book or a line? For a moment, the eyes of my eyes were opened ... There is no miracle so stupendous as this moment's health.

What Emerson was describing with these very words was an experience I had had one time in my life, an experience so thrilling it has remained with me all the years since as one of the most *alive* moments I have known.

At the time I was lying on a bed in an upstairs room in a home centuries-old in Saint-Cyprien, France. I was on vacation and was taking a much needed break from the steady flow of fine wine and food and over-indulgence. I especially wanted to finish my book, Virginia Woolf's *A Room of One's Own*. When I came upon the passage about "Shakespeare's sister" taking up residence in female writers, I was overcome by the very feelings Emerson describes. I was truly "bolted" to my feet and filled with such a surge of energy I could only pace about the room like an animal in a cage. The thing I remember most is standing at the window, so wholly elevated by the feelings that had possessed me, I felt I would burst right out of my body and fly out into the sky. That intense rush of feeling lasted only moments. And yet its effect on me was life-altering. I spent the next six years completely immersed in literature by women. In the seventh year, my first book *The Words of a Woman* came into being.

Gripping moments of inspiration are something I have experienced a handful of times in my life. I remember each of them in the same vivid detail as I recall the sensations of standing at that window that day in Saint-Cyprien. What is interesting to me now, looking back on them, is that they each prompted years of complete submersion in a creative process. And each time, though I had no idea where the process would lead, I was driven to follow it to its own end.

What is especially interesting is that until recently I would not have identified that first rapturous experience, reading *Emerson's Essays*, as one of those moments of inspiration. I did not think of it this way, you see, because it did not thrust me headlong into a creative process. It did not produce a creative work. I now see that without that moment the others would not have happened. I also see that though it took many years for me to begin this book, the process of creating it has been going on since that day in the grass all those years ago, reading Emerson.

I am now convinced that the very drive to create is a product of inspiration. It is perhaps the highest form of inspiration there is. For the aspiring writer it can carry with it years of frustration about how we will write and what we will write and how we will ever find our own voice. But if we feel in the depth of our soul that writing is what we must do, we should never lose sight of the fact that this in itself is a valuable thing. We have been given the most important calling we can have in this life — the desire to *create* something. Once it has made itself known to us, we need only keep ourselves open to continued inspiration. We need only keep a watchful eye for those "gleams of light which flash across the mind from within." And each time we are fortunate enough to have them reappear, as Emerson says — "yield to them heart and life."

Becoming a Writer

When the idea first came to me that I needed to write a book about writing, I honestly felt I would not need to do a single bit of research before beginning the process. I would be writing after all about the thing that has consumed me for a decade and a half and has given me as much joy as anything I have known. It was only a moment before it struck me as the peak of arrogance as well as stupidity to write such a book without reading some of the other books that are out there on the same subject, books other authors have been driven to write perhaps by the very same feelings.

The only books on writing I had read at that point were ones I had happened upon as I was delving literature by women, the process prompted by Virginia Woolf's "Shakespeare's sister." These books remain in my view some of the finest to recommend to aspiring writers, men and women alike — Virginia Woolf's *A Room of One's Own* and *A Writer's Diary*, Doris Lessing's *A Small Personal Voice*, Eudora Welty's *One Writer's Beginnings*, Willa Cather's *On Writing*, Annie Dillard's *A Writing Life*, and Brenda Ueland's *If You Want to Write*.

After reviewing a number of lists of "best books on writing," I read a good number of them. (Some I confess

I barely scanned while others I could not put down.) One of the things that struck me was how different each of the author's experiences were, becoming writers, and what each of them felt was important to recommend to aspiring writers. It was especially interesting to see that much of what was said about how to become a writer was not part of my experience at all.

Every single writer comes to writing in his or her own way. This is the most important thing any writer will tell you, that it really is your journey. What's more, it may take a whole lifetime to be able to look back with any understanding of your own journey. The key I believe is to try to understand early on that every writer's journey is unique — as yours will be. It will be unique to the person you are and to the gifts you have been given and to your particular experience of life. Most of all it will be *decided* by the commitment you make to it and by the passion you bring, especially for the long-term.

It would not be an exaggeration to say that I wanted to write from the time I was a young girl. By this I mean I was driven to creative expression as far back as I can remember. This took different forms over the years. When I was in my early twenties I recognized writing as my deepest aspiration. This was when I began journaling, which I did for many years. Volumes and volumes of random reflections, including my frustrations about finding the time to write. At the time I was convinced that this was the problem. Like everyone else I was busy building a life and making a living. I was busy becoming. Looking back now it is clear to me that for all those years the problem was not time. The problem was that I had not lived enough and learned enough to have any of my own ideas. Or perhaps more accurately, the ideas I did have I did not have the courage and the confidence to own. Most important, I had no form to give to the expression of my feelings, which was what the drive to write was really about for me.

It was not until years later that I read *A Room of One's Own*. And I am telling the absolute truth when I say that at the time I began *The Words of a Woman*, throughout the entire process, I had no idea what I was doing. I did not even know that what I was working toward was an eventual book. I truly was possessed. For six years I apportioned my time between professional work and creative work as religiously as others divide themselves between work and family. Evenings, weekends, vacations were all spent in my little apartment with the literary works of women strewn in piles on every surface including the floor. When I finished my "project," which was the only name I could give it at the time, my catharsis came in an unexpected form. Suddenly the dream I had carried all my life was something I could no longer ignore.

For years I had fantasized about taking my life-savings and moving to a cabin in the woods somewhere and "writing my guts out," as I used to say to my friends. "I just have to do it," I was always saying, "Life is too short." Well, I finally decided that it was time. I left my job and my income, my health insurance, all of the trappings of a "secure" life, and headed from Michigan to a little place in the redwoods of California where I had decided years earlier I wanted to experience the life of a writer. It was one of the most romantic, liberating, terrifying things I have ever done. I knew I had only enough money to support myself for a couple of years. What I would do after that, I had no idea. What was I going to write? I had a few ideas I hoped would take some form once I was able to focus on them. How would I be published? Would I be published? I could not think about that. My only real plan was to write for as long as I could and exactly what I needed to write.

On the way to California, somewhere around Wyoming, I launched into my prayer. "Please give me a sign that I am doing the right thing," I said. "If this really is my soul's true path, I'm going to need your help now. Please let me know that I'll somehow be able to support myself and live an authentic life." Right at that moment I found myself staring into a breathtaking sunset. It was as though the entire sky was filling up with God's resplendent answer to me. And wasn't that the way it was supposed to be, I thought. I had imagined the answer coming in just that kind of moment. The skies would part and all at once I would be assured that everything I needed would be provided for me. After all, I was following my bliss.

I have since learned that following one's bliss works like most other things in life. The skies do not part and the answer does not come in one stupendous moment. But the universe does rally around us. It supports us in profound ways. Not always in the ways we imagined. Not all the time. And not necessarily when we think we need it most. The universe is nothing if not creative. It communicates with us in astonishing ways — like that Wyoming sunset I will never forget. Six months after I moved to California I learned that *The Words of a Woman* was being picked up by a major publisher. Of course I knew that this was my sign. The proceeds were enough to support another year of writing. And this was the beginning of the succession of small miracles that have kept me writing for all the years since.

I would love to be able to tell you that through all these years I have felt entirely supported in my pursuit of my dream. I would love to be able to say there have been no major pitfalls along the way. But this is not the way the universe works. Not for most of us anyway. There have been many times during these past years when I have been absolutely terrified about how I would survive. Times when I have been so racked with fear and doubt I was sure I would rather die than face another day as a writer. And yet each time I have experienced these feelings I have been revived by another splendid moment, another small miracle that has helped me on my way.

The "soul's true path" is never an easy road. It can even be a difficult climb. It almost makes one wonder what God and the universe could possibly have had in mind, making the most important things in life so difficult to achieve. Or perhaps the challenges we face in pursuing a meaningful life are not really obstacles at all. Perhaps they are an important part of the process.

Looking back now, I see the universe's boundless perfection even in my own little life. I see that I was not emotionally prepared to devote myself to writing until precisely when I did. I see that twenty years of journaling, frustrations and all, was part of my journey and one of the most impactful processes of my spiritual and emotional life. I see that the skills I honed through decades of professional work have proved invaluable to my writing. And most important, I have learned as much from the difficult times as I have from the splendid moments. And this, I believe is the way the universe works.

What is important to point out about my particular experience is that through all those years of journaling, I experienced only the frustrations of an aspiring writer. I had no idea how I would ever manage the time for serious writing or how I would ever know what to write. It was not until that moment with Virginia Woolf's "Shakespeare's sister," the moment I was completely overtaken by a creative impulse with a life of its own, that I instinctively committed myself to writing. The other thing that is important to emphasize again is that this was my experience. Yours will be entirely different because it will be yours.

Yes, there are many good books out there that may be helpful to you as you pursue your writing. What is important to remember is that every single one of them represents one writer's experience, one writer's perspective. If they speak of what you must do to become a writer, they are speaking of what worked for them. They are sharing what they have come to view as the best advice they can give. Books about writing are also not all about the same thing. Some are about the craft of writing, about tools and rules and techniques. Some are for aspiring journalists or people who want to build careers as writers. Some are good reference books to keep around for when you have specific questions about the mechanics of writing. Some are about strategies for getting published or formulas for writing a successful novel. There are many different books that may hold some value for you. But only you can decide which ones those are — first, for the aspiring creative writer — and then, specifically, for you. Chances are you will find that the best books to help you become a creative writer are not books about writing at all, they are just great books.

Is it possible to learn how to write creatively? To be trained as a creative writer? In response to this question I am always reminded of a story I once read about Katherine Anne Porter standing before a group of aspiring writers at Sarah Lawrence College. As the story goes, she looked out at her audience and said, "If you want to write, what are you doing here? Go home and write!" This, of course, was Katherine Anne Porter's experience. She learned to write on her own. On the question of how you should go about learning to write — just as with each of those students in that lecture hall that day — only you can decide what is right for you.

There are many good writers who will tell you that it is important to learn to write, that it was the most valuable thing they did, pursuing their writing through a fine creative writing program. Others will tell you how much they regret not having formal training, how much they wish they could have avoided all of the trial and error and the struggles they endured, learning to write in their own self-imposed vacuum. Still others will say that formal training won't help you one bit, that it may even stifle your "pilgrim soul."

All any of us can speak to is our own experience. My experience has been such that I could only be fascinated by some of the specific advice given by writers for how to go about becoming a writer. Fascinated, in part, because if I had read some of those books early on I could only have been discouraged from following my own instincts. I could only have been held back on my particular path. As I read some of those recommendations I could not help feeling that what every aspiring writer needs to hear is that they may decide to do none of those things. They may even deliberately avoid those things, as well as the idea that any of them are important.

Fortunately, I did follow my instincts and completely avoided anyone else's thoughts on how to become a writer. I never took a writing course or attended a writers' workshop or built a support network of other writers or submitted articles to magazines. And until very recently I never read a book about writing that provided me with anything but pure inspiration. In my case, I knew there was only one way to pursue my own writing and that was to bury myself for years and to write.

Have I struggled any more than any other aspiring writer committed to her own creative work? I don't believe I have. The truth is I could not be happier about the particular way I have gone about it. (Or the way it has gone about me.) If I had the opportunity to do it over I would not change a thing about my experience, including having more training or more support in the areas where I needed it most. I would even tell you that the trial and error, the major blunders, the painful struggles, have not only been a valuable part of the process, they have been essential *to* the process, the process of *learning* to write, the process of *becoming* a writer.

If it sounds as though I would be one of those who would discourage you from pursuing a creative writing program — I am the last person who would discourage anyone from any kind of learning. If a creative writing program is what you choose to do, you could only learn a great deal. This is what I believe any responsible person would tell you — that what makes the difference in any learning experience is that it is self-directed. This is no doubt what any writing teacher would tell you too.

If it sounds as though I would advocate the Katherine Anne Porter approach, to simply "go home and write"— I would not do that either. I would encourage you to carefully assess what is right for you. Of course I enjoy the Katherine Anne Porter story, because that is what worked for me. And because I am convinced it is the only way that would have worked for me. Some would say it did not even work for me, that I am not a successful writer. I can only tell you that I have succeeded beyond my own imaginings. For the past fifteen years I have been able to wake up every day and look forward to writing. And what I have learned in the process has made every bit of struggle worthwhile.

As Emerson said, "There is no way to learn to write except by writing." The fact is that we all learn to write by writing, however we go about it. What Emerson said that I believe is important for every aspiring writer to hear is this: "Those who have written best are not those who have known most, but those to whom writing was natural and necessary." If writing is natural and necessary to you, you will learn to write in your own way. You will become a writer in the way that is natural to you.

Finding Your Voice

"The way to speak and write that shall not go out of fashion is to speak and write sincerely."

"Finding your voice" is an expression every writer understands whether we've been writing for half an hour or half a century. I don't believe any writer ever stops trying to find her voice. This is part of what keeps even the greatest writers writing. They are always digging deeper within themselves, trying to uncover deeper truths, trying to express themselves in their most authentic voice.

What I believe we are all really searching for as we strive to find our own voice is courage. We are trying to find the courage we know we possess. Courage to listen to the voice within us, to trust that it has value, to express what is ours to express. What we are really trying to find is the courage to be ourselves.

One of the many things that years of writing teaches us is that it is impossible to separate our writing life from our life. What we learn from our life infuses our writing and what we learn from our writing informs our life. What both teach us, when we are really paying attention, is that we can only be who we are. The moment we start comparing ourselves to someone else, the moment we try to be like someone else, we rob ourselves of the most precious thing we have, which is the opportunity to be who we are, to speak in the voice that is uniquely ours. As Emerson would say, we rob ourselves of the "the joy of uttering what no other can utter."

Whenever we find ourselves saying, "This is great writing," it is because we have eagerly read every word an author has written and heard her as though she were speaking directly to us. What we hear most of all is that she is standing squarely on her own two feet and being exactly who she is.

Two of the books on writing I most enjoyed were Anne Lamott's *Bird by Bird* and Stephen King's *On Writing* — both bestsellers and also listed on the must-read lists for people who want to write. *Bird by Bird* I recalled a friend mentioning to me years ago; I now understand why. And I read Stephen King's book because I thought it was important to have the perspective of an extremely popular author — and who wouldn't want to know how Stephen King's mind works? As it turned out these were two of the books I could not put down. I would recommend them not only to every aspiring writer but to anyone and everyone, as they are also great books about life. (Aren't all great books books about life.) They both also gave me something that "high graders" don't always get in our reading — the opportunity to laugh out loud. Repeatedly. Truly. They are both great reads.

Anne Lamott and Stephen King are very different from one another. They write different kinds of books, have had different life experiences, different experiences becoming writers. But what most comes through in both of their writing, what makes them good writers as well as popular ones, is that they are who they are. This is perhaps the most valuable thing any writer will tell you — about writing and about life. True, deep honesty is a difficult thing to achieve, even with ourselves. And yet the only way for any of us to touch that spark of genius inside us is to be exactly who we are.

Why does it take so much courage to be who we are and to speak in the voice that is ours? If you have not yet experienced fear in relation to writing, in relation to saying what *you* have to say, you have probably not yet begun to write. And if you think you have overcome all your fear in relation to writing, you are probably not writing anymore. Part of the job of writing is overcoming fear. Every time we think we have completed the job, sheer terror seizes us again. I don't believe I have experienced more paralyzing fear than I have as a writer. Fear I would have previously imagined only in response to a life-threatening event. And I don't believe there is a single writer who would not say the same thing.

Emerson said, "He has not learned the lessons of life who does not every day surmount a fear." Perhaps he even chose his life's work based on his Aunt Mary's advice to him: "Always do what you are afraid to do." I believe Emerson would tell us that fear is part of what drives the creative process. The important thing is to remain driven by it.

I now understand a little better why it is such a struggle for writers to get at our own simple truths, to express our thoughts and feelings just as they are. We know that if we do we will be putting ourselves out there in front of the world as the bare naked souls we are. We will be exposing ourselves in ways that will enable people to hurt us, because they will know our greatest weaknesses and how much a part of us they really are.

When we write, when we commit our thoughts and ideas to writing, even before our words are published, even if they are never published, what we are doing essentially is giving ourselves away. We are saying, "This is who I am and what I have to give, what I think and feel and believe is important." And though it may have come from the very heart of us — it may have come with as much hard work and suffering as if we had given birth — once a thing is written, it no longer belongs to us. It belongs to the world. It belongs to every person who wishes to make it their own, to express their opinion about it, to even make it over to their own interpretation.

Every one of us knows this instinctively every moment we are writing. We know we are engaged in the act of giving ourselves away. We even know we may be exposing ourselves in ways we do not intend. In ways it will be up to others to decide. What we are most afraid of is that someone in their criticism of what we have written will happen upon one of our deepest vulnerabilities, the ones we work hard to keep hidden in our everyday lives. This is one of the most valuable things that can come to us through writing. We can actually come to identify our own deep fears. We can even come to terms with the ones that are most holding us back.

In my case it was my feeling of inferiority about my level of education. This was my greatest fear as a writer. I was afraid that if I expressed myself in my most honest voice, if I gave up my honest truths, I might sound as uneducated as I feared I was. What finally came to me was that my fear of being uneducated is the most valuable thing I have. It is the quality I would least want to be without. By another name it might be called "the drive to learn." The truth is that I have had a wonderful education, entirely self-directed and exhilarating every step of the way. What's more, I have one of the hungriest minds I have personally known. Hungry for knowledge and for experience and for living every day an examined life. My real insecurity came from the fact that I do not have the credentials that a highly credentialed person could point to as a weakness in me. They could easily dismiss what I have to say, you see, by pointing to my inferior education.

The truth is, we all care about credentials. I look for them all the time. Because most of the reading I do is research, it is fuel for my writing, I am comforted when I see a PhD after an author's name — and from an Ivy League school even better! Though it goes against my fundamental grain to place value on credentials, there are times when they mean a great deal. They assure me that the chances are increased that my ultimate thoughts on a subject will be well-supported. On the other hand, when I am seeking great literature or philosophy or spiritual enrichment, do I give a moment's care to an author's degrees? Emerson is a good example. I have read and revered him all my life and it was not until recently that I knew anything about his education. As I learned, Emerson was indeed formally educated but he placed the highest value on his own independent learning. He also had some wonderful insights about education which have helped me immensely as I have dealt with my insecurities as a thinker and writer.

The other realization that came to me was — who does not feel the same way? Who is not afraid they will be dismissed as not educated enough or not "smart" enough by someone more educated or smarter than they are? I can only imagine that the more educated a person is, the greater his concern that someone will find holes in his knowledge. Who does not fear in the deepest part of himself that he will be judged as somehow *less* than someone else?

What I found so very interesting as I was reading my collection of books on writing is that I sensed in some writers the same level of discomfort, not about being undereducated but about being highly educated, especially when they were educated as creative writers. Some even seem a bit resentful of what they feel is a bias among readers and publishers toward the writer who has no training at all, who essentially stumbles out of the wilderness and writes a great book. (While the writer in the wilderness is of course convinced of a very different reality!) What these authors' comments made me see is that being formally educated carries a whole other set of expectations that untrained writers never face. And they are not only imposed by the people who hold the keys to the literary world, and the people who offer admittance to that world through our university programs, but also by the writer herself who wrestles with those expectations every day.

We all have unwanted voices in our heads, no matter our background or training or experience. We have voices in our heads that get in our way. As different as they may be for each of us, they all have one thing in common: they have nothing to do with us. They are about what other people think and what other people value and what other people will say. And they get in the way of our own clear passage to what it is that we have to say.

What is it about writing that makes it such a challenge to tune out all other voices and get at our own authentic voice? Don't we all speak in our own authentic voice every day? "Authentic," of course, means "genuine," "sincere." And as we dig deeper into its origins we find phrases like "of undisputed origin," and "acting on one's own authority." An authentic voice, a voice that rests on its own authority, is a self-reliant voice. It has nothing to do with anyone outside ourselves. What we discover when we begin to write is that self-reliance is not something any of us has learned. We have in fact learned quite the opposite. We all have other voices in our heads all the time. They only become so loud and obnoxious when we begin to write.

And what is this "truth" that writers are always talking about? What do we mean when we say that "artists are driven by the search for truth," or that we are "trying to get at the truth that is ours to express." We have all learned that it is arrogant to believe we can know truth. One of the reasons is that we tend to confuse truth with knowledge. When we understand as Emerson did that truth emerges not in the mind but in the soul, we realize how equal we all are in relation to truth. We all come into contact with valuable truths every day.

"Truth" can take the form of a single insight to human nature, or to the mysteries of life, or even to the nature of truth. Such insights are given new expression every day in all forms of art, including all forms of literature. As Emerson said, "Literature is the record of all; the sum and measure of humanity ...

> Every part of man has its department in literature; his observation, in history; his love, in lyrics and novels; his wrath in satire and controversies; his mirth in comedy; his piety in psalms and sermons; his contemplation in philosophy. Even crime and folly have their books ... Thus it represents all human thought ... and fixes the divine boundaries of the human spirit.

Creative writing — writing that makes us feel we are somehow *more* for having read it — this kind of writing can take many different forms. It is not the form that makes creative writing but what the writing achieves. Is it possible to contribute to "the sum and measure of humanity" through even page-turning, popular forms? I can only imagine that popular authors ask themselves this question every day.

No one recognized better than Emerson that the real truth-tellers, the truth-revealers, come along once every century or two. These are the "minds nearest the stars" who not only fix the divine boundaries of the human spirit, they redefine and expand them. What Emerson stressed repeatedly is that the great thinkers and writers had no more insight to truth than any one of us. What set them apart was their trust in their insights, and their drive to give them full expression.

Emerson would tell us that the desire to find our voice goes hand in hand with the desire to know truth. He would urge us to reject the idea that either of these things is difficult to achieve. He believed that each of us has our own natural voice, one that is not entirely under our control, and that when we are "not thinking of it, it will always assume." Most important, he believed that "the more truly we consult our own powers" the more distinct our voice will be. As for discovering truths and trusting our own insights to truth, he said —

> We know the truth when we see it, let skeptic or scoffer say what they choose ...
> We know the truth ... as we know when we are awake that we are awake.

We all know instinctively that the key to finding our voice is to trust entirely in what comes to us from within. Unfortunately, this is something most of us are able to do only in moments. As writers, we learn to seize those moments. We learn that in those moments we are able to simply be ourselves, to trust what we feel called to say, to say it in our own way. We even find that we are able to forgive ourselves for the times we are filled with fear. We realize that we cannot feel trust every day any more than the universe can give us signs every day. After a while, we learn to simply trust that we will trust again.

Just yesterday, as I was writing this chapter, I was suddenly overcome with fear and doubt — even about the value of this project, which has flowed from me as naturally as anything I have written. What happened was that I began comparing myself again to people far smarter than I am, people I imagined finding little worth in what I have to say. I had not experienced those feelings since the day I began this project and it was disheartening to have them reappear. Fortunately, I have had enough experience with them now to know they also disappear. So I pushed myself away from my computer and said, "You're just plain sick of your voice today, Christine. Give yourself a day away. Tomorrow will be a good day." And so it is.

Shutting Out the Other Voices

*"It is easy to live for others; everybody does.
I call on you to live for yourselves."*

No matter who we are, no matter what we bring to writing, much of the work of finding our voice is shutting out other voices. Emerson was a master at this. His ability to shut out all voices except the ones he valued was part of what made him the force he was. As John Jay Chapman saw it, this was "the secret of his stimulating power." "Emerson knows we are full of genius," he said, "and that we have only to throw something off, not to acquire any new thing."

We all need to "throw off" other voices that become especially intrusive when we are trying to get at ours. For some reason it is rarely our "ideal reader" we hear the most from. It is the reader who is thoroughly unimpressed with what we have to say, who may even dismiss or attack what we have to say. That reader haunts every writer. He hovers in our consciousness and continually invades our thoughts. He erodes our confidence in even our most determined thoughts. If we don't call him out and dismiss him for what he is, he can have a paralyzing effect.

> What I must do is all that concerns me, not what the people think ... Do your work, and you shall reinforce yourself.

This was the attitude I tried to adopt when I committed to writing. I needed to shut out all other voices, you see, because I knew they would cripple me if I concerned myself with them. I knew there was enough of a critic in my own head to have to deal with every day. This is the only critic any of us needs to concern our self with. This is the real opponent that stands in our way. It helps if we can recognize that this particular voice is our own creation. It is the voice we give to our fears and doubts and feelings of inadequacy. And just as we have the power to create it, we have the power to tune it out. We even have the power to wrestle down the untruths it continually spews at us. Unfortunately, for most of us, these are things we must do over and over again.

There is another voice that plagues every aspiring writer that is especially difficult to shut out — the one that talks incessantly about "success." "How will you be published?" it asks us. "How will you make sense out of years of writing without some tangible evidence of success?" It won't let us forget that succeeding is an important thing. It is not only important for us but for the people who believe in us. How can we be worthy of their support and their love if we don't somehow succeed?

There is one perspective that I believe is important for every creative writer to have from the start and to try to hold onto every day: We are doing the kind of work that makes it a laudable thing to hope for commercial success, to hope that millions of people the world over will read and appreciate what we have written. And yet it is just this kind of writing to which there is little use attaching such dreams. The truth is that the only measures of success we will ever be able to hold ourselves to are the ones we create for ourselves.

My dream when I began writing was to earn enough money to be able to continue writing. This truly was my highest hope. When I learned my first book would be published, I of course fantasized that I had found my way to a successful path, that I would be able to support myself as a writer. I even had visions of future successes that far exceeded the realities that came. But the truth is my dream never changed. Being able to write was all I asked. Would I like to feel rewarded and acknowledged and materially compensated for all my hard work? Of course I would. But what I wanted most is the thing that came. I have been able to continue writing.

If this sounds lofty and pretentious to you, I understand. It sounds lofty and pretentious to me too when it is put into words. But I assure you the feeling is real. By every standard that is presented to us as a measure of success in American society, I have not been a successful writer. One could even say I have worked very hard for a long time with little to show for it. That is because the most significant thing I have gained as a writer is not something that can be seen on any pages. It is what I have learned in the process — about myself, about life, about the creative process, and about this fascinating affliction, the urge to write.

Emerson said, "Happy is he who looks only into his work to know if it will succeed ... and who writes from the love of imparting certain thoughts and not from the necessity of sale." These sentiments are utterly foreign to our American way of thinking. They are also not easy ones to achieve. But if we look closely at this statement of Emerson's we see that with these few words he liberates us entirely from anyone else's measures of success. He also assures us that our own sense of success is something we can create for ourselves.

When Emerson was eighteen, he confided to his Aunt Mary his "dream-like anticipations of greatness." He and his aunt both knew he was destined for greatness. For Emerson this was about something so much larger than personal success. It was about reaching the greatest heights in the world of thought, in the world of ideas. This was Emerson's dream. To live a rich inner life. *To write for the love of imparting certain thoughts.* His dream like anticipations of greatness had nothing to do with worldly success.

Emerson's books for the first fifteen years they were in print were referred to by his publishers as "very poor paying stock." It took twelve years to sell five hundred copies of *Nature*. Yes, he eventually became successful enough as a lecturer to support his family and have a decent life. But based on the early success of his books could he ever have dreamed that they would one day be widely read all over the world? That he would become a seminal figure in American thought? Lawrence Buell says "Emerson never seems to have given a moment's thought to the prospect of permanent fame. He would almost surely have been surprised by the durability of his canonization."

"Fame" is another measure of success that is difficult to shut out of our minds, especially as Americans. And yet, in today's America, what is "fame?" It is achieved through nothing more than notoriety, controversy, even outrageousness. It need not be earned through any achievement or have any affirmative value at all. Emerson's day was of course not exempt from this kind of thinking. Emerson's controversial "Divinity School Address" sold a hundred times more quickly than *Nature*. But imagine someone being famous in America today, drawing crowds of people everywhere he went, because of his passion for ideas and his gift for inspiring conscious thought in his listeners. Imagine someone becoming famous as "the friend and aider of those who would live in the spirit."

Surely every one of us in some secret place within our self is attracted by the idea of being *known* — especially for some creative expression of our self. And yet if the trends in American culture tell us anything, they tell us that being widely known is not something to aspire to. As creative writers, what we need to ask ourselves is — In what company do we wish to be known? What kind of readers do we hope to reach with our writing? This is the group we want to hold in our minds whenever we imagine some level of "fame." And it is more than okay that it ends up being a very small group.

Emerson did enjoy some of the privileges of fame during his lifetime. But he took great pains not to be drawn in by it, and as he said, "out of equilibrium." He recognized that "society's praise can be cheaply secured" and that fame "puts one into a false position in relation to others." Most important, "it spoils thought."

I believe Emerson would tell us to absolutely strive for greatness in our writing. But greatness determined not by the world around us but by the world within. He would tell us that the deepest agony comes not from being deprived of commercial success but from not achieving real success, the success we hold in our own minds. In other words, he would tell us to simply concentrate on *growing good corn*.

> If a man has good corn, or wood ... or can make better chairs or knives ... than anybody else, you will find a broad, hard-beaten road to his house, though it be in the woods ... Well, it is still so with a thinker. If he proposes to show me a high human secret ... all good heads, and all mankind religiously wish to know it ... and his fame will surely be bruited abroad.

If what we are focused on while we are writing is the image of a broad beaten path to our door, or any other worldly acknowledgement or reward — Emerson says No.

This is not the way to grow good corn. We must give ourselves wholly to the quality of the corn itself, to achieving a taste and texture that satisfies *us*. He would also tell us, as no doubt any good corn-grower would, that good corn can take years to achieve.

There are of course those who will tell us that there are standard, objective measures of greatness in writing. There are experts who can tell us whether they have been met or not and why. But each of those experts has his or her own ideas about what makes great writing. And each will not use the same standards of measure with any two writers. They will not describe the gifts of Jane Austen, for instance, in the same terms they apply to the merits of Mark Twain. What makes Proust great is not the same as that which makes Hemingway popular. What I believe the very best literary critics would tell us is that the single thing that can be said of every great writer is that they wrote what was theirs to write. They would also acknowledge that what makes writing great to any of us is that it speaks to us.

When we read, when we engage in that wonderful relationship between author and reader, we are able to shut out all other voices and focus on what the author is saying to us. Why is it that when we are writing we must continually work at silencing other voices? And it is not just the ones we create out of our own fears. It is every voice we have ever taken in that had something to say about what makes good writing. Some of them can sound so authoritative, we forget that another voice, an equally creditable voice, might tell us something entirely different.

As I was reading my collection of books on writing I came across a number of those authoritative voices, the ones that can get lodged in an aspiring writer's head only to make the job of finding one's voice even more challenging. One writer was so specific he cited particular words and phrases that writers should never use. I won't tell you what they were because then I'd be lodging them in your head to be stumbling blocks forever. I will tell you they were all words and phrases I read and write all the time, some I rather like. Likes and dislikes for words and phrases are entirely subjective things. I personally think that no word should be banned from use by writers and I am confident that any great writer would tell us the same thing.

This is of course an example of a very small stumbling block. There are much larger ones that can be terribly intimidating to beginning writers and remain in their way for a long time. Anyone who has read a single one of the vast majority of books on writing has another voice that haunts him — the one that tells us to always use as few words as possible, to "cut to the quick" in our use of language. Today this is a commonly accepted rule of writing. And yet such rules only make things more difficult for the writer who is struggling to get at her own voice, struggling to believe that such a thing exists. She might even interpret this one to mean she should never write a long sentence. And how is she to learn how she expresses herself when she is always afraid the next word might be too much? I was personally thrilled by a comment in Roy Peter Clark's book *Writing Tools* that I thought every aspiring writer should hear: "Everyone fears the long sentence. Editors fear it. Readers fear it. Most of all, writers fear it … Write what you fear. Until the writer tries to master the long sentence, she is no writer at all, for while length makes a bad sentence worse, it can make a good sentence better."

Emerson too said, "Amputate. Amputate! … Drop adjectives and let the noun do the work! … Say it! Out with it! Search unweariedly for that which is exact!" And yet some would say Emerson was the most longwinded writer who ever lived. Emerson's greatest advice to writers we find not in anything he said about writing but in the uniqueness of his own style. He expressed himself in the way that was natural to him, without regard for anyone's ideas about what makes good writing.

But the idea that I believe is most intimidating, especially to enthusiastic young writers, is another one that is ever-present in our discourse on writing, which is the disparagement of sentiment. When we disparage "sentimentalism," after all, this is what we are disparaging — sentiment. We are so frightening young writers away from writing anything with feeling in it for fear it will be perceived as merely "sentimental." I saw this word so repeatedly recently I wanted to understand why it is given such attention. And that is the irony. It is constantly talked about in dismissive terms.

Objections to "sentimentalism" are often couched in terms that would lead one to believe it is an absolute given among intelligent people that reason and intelligence are to be valued above feelings and emotions. This is in fact one side of an argument that has been with us since the dawn of thought. An argument that has some highly intelligent people on the other side. Emerson trusted his feelings above his thoughts. As Gay Wilson Allen put it, for Emerson "truth was more felt than thought out." Or as John Dewey expressed it, "To Emerson, perception was more potent than reasoning." Evelyn Barish even goes so far as to say that for Emerson "the origin of his knowledge lay in human feeling."

No one placed a higher value on an intellectual life than Emerson. He thought from the time he rose until the time he slept. And yet to Emerson the role of the intellect was merely one of supporting the passage of truth through one's expression — truth that comes to us through "the intellects shy younger sister, *sentiment*." Of course we want to give feelings the dignity they deserve and present them with intelligence. We want to carefully avoid counterfeit emotions — counterfeit anything! But we should never allow anyone else's discomfort with emotions to dissuade us from valuing *feelings*. There are far too many of them we all share.

Emerson believed we should not only place a high value on feelings, we should bring to our writing the very height of feeling — enthusiasm. "Enthusiasm" (or "God in us") is an upward, forward kind of feeling that is especially devalued in our society. We learn this at an early age. When we were young kids in school and read a poem or a piece of prose, who were the students who were perceived as the "smartest?" The ones who were filled with enthusiasm about it, who "loved" it and thought it was "great?" Or the ones who criticized it mercilessly, pointing out its every flaw? We learn early that to be enthusiastic, to be passionate and full of feeling, is not the way to be perceived as "smart."

> What is a man good for without enthusiasm? ... All excellence is only an inflamed personality ... Be the fanatic of your subject, and find a fibre reaching from it to the core of your heart ... Nothing great was ever achieved without enthusiasm.

The point is that when it comes to ideas about what makes good writing there is always someone equally gifted who would tell us something different than those commanding voices that get stuck in our heads. The ones that only create more fear in us about our own honest expression.

And what about the real-life critics who live in our heads? The ones whose voices we also hear the entire time we are writing? For most of us the most daunting ones are those of family or friends, teachers, mentors, nemeses from childhood — people who are permanently embedded in our psyches. Those voices can be as intrusive as any other force we face. And it is pointless to imagine we could ever really tune them out. Part of the challenge of writing, I'm convinced, is embracing those voices as integral to who we are and to what we have to say. This is one of the other valuable things that can come to us through writing. We can come to understand those forces and how powerful they are. We can even achieve some perspective on them that can only come to us through writing.

If the voices of literary critics, real or imagined, are ones we carry in our heads, we either have some experience with them or we have high hopes for commercial success. Of all the voices to give the boot, these should be the first to go. And not just because most of us will never face real public criticism of our work but because anticipating it is as counter-productive as anything we can do. It is not only not self-reliant, it is as far a reach outside ourselves as we can get.

When we are truly committed to finding our own way as writers there is another voice we must keep shut out of our consciousness. The one that says we are only serious writers if we turn out new books with a certain regularity. This is a voice that is especially important for creative writers to tune out. If we don't, we can't possibly give to each project the time it deserves. As Annie Dillard said, "It takes years to write a book — between two and ten years ... Out of the human population on earth," she says, "perhaps twenty people can write a book in a year. Some people lift cars too." I loved Annie Dillard for saying that. After years of tuning out that particular voice, here was a gift from a serious writer.

Shutting out all voices except the ones we value — this is one of the most important things we do as writers.

And it is important to make this commitment early on. Otherwise, we spend our time battling endless voices instead of doing our work.

When Emerson said (in Chapman's words) "we only have to throw something off," he was talking about something he knew only too well. Criticism, controversy, family angst, misunderstanding, every form of external expectation! — these are things that followed Emerson in the greatest extremes all his life. Emerson of course had the great advantage of a mind so filled with ideas, so bent on expressing them, the unwanted voices were easily crowded out. But his greatest strength, his greatest defense against all intrusive forces, I'm convinced, was another quality I am sure he would point to as the absolute key.

For me it was expressed most poignantly in something he wrote in his journal the day he met Mary Rotch, the Quaker woman from New Bedford who was another of those brief encounters in his life that turned out to be a powerful source of illumination. He was so impressed by their conversation he gave a faithful account of it as he reflected on it. Mary Rotch had told him that for her, true faith was the faith she found in the deepest part of herself, the faith that "the dissent of all mankind could not shake, and which the consent of all mankind could not confirm."

This, Emerson would tell us is the final test that must be applied to anything we write. When we find ourselves working hard at shutting out other voices, it is because we have not yet arrived at the place where we can truly own our own truths. When we do, we know *they can neither be shaken nor confirmed by anyone else.* They may be enriched by others. And we may even be hurt by having them misunderstood or dismissed. But our faith in them remains unchanged. As does our delight at having discovered them.

Tilling Your Plot of Ground

Years ago I sat across from a man at a dinner who made his living as a writer. As I recall he wrote for a number of magazines and did his own creative work on the side. I was young then and quite dreamy-eyed, I'm sure, as I looked at him and said, "Oh, I want to write." He looked at me as though he might pick up his water glass and pitch it at someone. I was a little afraid it might be me. Clearly, he was painfully accustomed to hearing the same thing from virtually every person he met. He took a moment and composed himself and then he said, "Well, when writing becomes a reality for you, you'll find out it's damn hard work. Mind-battering, gut-wrenching, back-breaking work."

I have never forgotten that man. I even wish I could tell him today how much I understand his reaction to me then. We all begin with romantic notions about writing, I think. Until we begin to write. What we discover is that we not only have to find and stake out our own "plot of ground" — we have to work it.

What goes into the work of writing? To begin with, the same things that invite inspiration — long periods of solitude, creative reading, time with Nature, life experience, and deep conversation with true friends. These are the things that bring ideas to the surface for us and begin to give them form. What else goes into the tilling and the toil involved in writing? Unfortunately, there is not a writer alive who will not tell us the same thing that man told me years ago — more physical, mental and emotional hard work than most people would ever imagine.

> Can you ... sail a ship through the Narrows by minding the helm when you happen to think of it ... or accomplish anything good ... or powerful in this manner?... And the greatest of all arts, the subtlest, and of most miraculous effect, you fancy is to be practiced with a pen in one hand and a crowbar or a peat-knife in the other ... The writer must live and die by his writing. Good for that and good for nothing else.

The ability to live and die by our writing, as Emerson put it, is not something any of us comes by easily. The physical and psychic space in which to do nothing but write for extended periods — this alone is a huge challenge. For one thing, unless we have some reliable long-term support, we spend far too much time worrying about how we will get by. Talk about voices we can't get out of our heads. How about the one that says, "You have to eat and take care of your family!" We all have to support ourselves, we have families, we have lives. Even if we are willing to give up some portion of these things, it is still a struggle. And yet if the drive to write is great enough we do what every writer who ever lived did, even in the face of overwhelming challenges. We carve out the time and space we need to write what we need to write.

Many writers say that the way to make time for writing is to discipline oneself to write a certain amount of time each day and write every day without fail. They say that no matter our circumstances, time for writing is achieved through discipline. I have a little different read on this idea about the discipline writing requires, perhaps due entirely to my own experience — or perhaps because I really am a nutcase as many of my family and friends would attest. The only discipline I have ever needed since the day I committed to writing is the energy I must sometimes give to pulling myself away from writing. If you are a nutcase too, once a particular project takes hold of you, you won't need to think about discipline or schedules or anything else. You will write every minute you possibly can. The key, I believe, is to begin writing when you feel you must. When you feel, as Emerson said, that "you shall perish if you do not."

The next thing that is required for writing is something even beyond the opportunity for solitude; it is an actual penchant for it. We need to be comfortable being alone for hours on end. As Emerson said, we must "embrace solitude as a bride." If you are truly driven to creative writing you are probably also a person who finds that you need a certain amount of alone time. You likely feel that the time you spend alone is an important part of your life.

Real solitude, the solitude it takes for any creative work, not only requires a lot from us internally, it requires a great deal from us as social beings as well. "Society and Solitude" was more than the theme of a series of lectures in Emerson's life. He was continually torn between the two, as every creative writer must be. As Vivian Hopkins said, It is "the paradox which confronts every writer: how to satisfy the human demands of family and friends, so necessary to thought as to life, and yet manage to get work done."

As ironic as it may seem, the other fundamental necessity that goes hand in hand with solitude *is* society, the society of the people we love, the people who make it hard for us to hole up for hours away from them. It is the people in our lives who support our writing that make writing possible for us. This is why so many writers dedicate their books to their spouses. Having a partner who is also our partner in our pursuit of our dream, the dream we hold "like an insanity" — this is everything. When I referred to the small miracles that have kept me writing — most of those miracles have come in the form of relationships. Without the particular people in my life, especially my husband, I would not have been able to continue writing as I have. Even more important, I would not have experienced the amazing feeling that the person I love most, the person closest to me, is as invested in my writing as I am. This is the greatest miracle in any writer's life.

And there is another important role that the irreplaceable people in our lives play in our writing. We all need at least one person, preferably a few, who are our first readers of everything we write. People with whom we share unconditional love and respect, whose thoughts we value, who we know will be honest with us in their response to our work and even care enough to be specific. Those few trusted friends in my life, including my husband, have become so invaluable to my work I have actually come to view my first-draft exchanges with them as a vital step in the creative process.

Sharing our work for the first time with another person — this is one of the more difficult things we do as writers. It is kind of like taking our clothes off and saying "what do you think?" And yet some of the most valuable things that come to our writing can come through the process of doing just that, exposing our work when it is still in a formative stage, when we know instinctively that it is time to bring someone else into the process. The people we choose to do this with need to be people we trust implicitly and people we value as participants in our own creative processing. Because that is what they are. They are actual participants. They can even take the process to brand new heights.

I am convinced that a significant part of the desire to write is the desire to express what we need to express to the people in our lives. This is part of our objective, always, to share our thoughts and feelings with the people who will really hear us, who will find in our expression that deeply personal part of our selves that we yearn to share. It is amazing what happens when some of those same people offer their keen eyes and ears to what we have written. Of course we must eventually move beyond our "ideal reader," as Stephen King calls her (for him also, his spouse.) But we all need a support system of intimate confidantes for that first leap outside ourselves.

One of those faithful friends in my life, Robert Klaus, died of Parkinson's before I was able to share this book with him. Losing Robert was one of the greatest losses I have known. And not being able to share this particular book with him will remain one of my greatest disappointments. Robert was one of those friends years ago with whom I regularly commiserated about how difficult it is to live our lives at the same time we pursue meaningful lives. He understood the deep urge to write as well as anyone I have known. When I finally took the leap and abandoned my sensible life for a creative one, he made me feel I was giving him the vicarious thrill of a lifetime. He has made me feel that way through all the years since. No one was more interested to see the outcome of my years immersed in Emerson than Robert.

Robert would have appreciated my thoughts on the great value of "reading up." I only hope he knows that because of the great good fortune of having him in my life

I have also had the experience of writing up. I have been writing up for years. We "write up" when the most enormous presence in our head the entire time we are writing is the most brilliant person we know. This is perhaps the most valuable advice I am able to give you as an aspiring writer — Include among your first readers those you are proudest to have in your life.

If the reader will indulge me one more personal moment with my friend — My heart is filled with the Yeats sentiment that we invoked with one another many times — "And say my glory was I had such friends."

This is of course the society that matters most to any of us, the people closest to us. And yet as Emerson made clear, the creative writer must also care about the larger society of which he is part. He must even take responsibility for his own contribution to it. This is where Emerson confronted his greatest conflict. He was constantly torn not just between the people he loved and the solitude that was so essential to his work but also between his responsibilities as an American citizen, a citizen of the world, and his devotion to the world of ideas. As Ralph Rusk said, he "gave up any debate on the spirit of the times in favor of eternal questions." Questions about the meaning of life, about the right way for a man to live, even about how to live in the world without being of the world.

Emerson is known for his vociferous opposition to slavery at a time when such voices were just emerging in our nation. To Emerson, it was the responsibility of the scholar to not only speak up on important social issues but to be on the right side of them. "A scholar defending the cause of slavery," he said, "is a traitor to his profession." Emerson was pulled into a number of national debates that he simply could not turn away from. And yet, as Lawrence Buell points out, even at the height of the Civil War Emerson was vacillating between the crisis that raged around him and his reading of Confucius and Upanishads and Sufi mysticism. He was caught in the "solitude *vs.* society" battle that was so much a part of his life.

One of the major discrepancies among the Transcendentalists in fact was this very divide between thinking vs. doing. For a number of Emerson's friends the movement was about activism. It was about bringing about important social reforms. For Margaret Fuller, it was about the rights of women; for Bronson Alcott, education. And though Thoreau was the most reclusive of them all, the most given to an inner life, he could easily be named America's first environmental advocate, as well as our foremost proponent of *Civil Disobedience.*

Emerson resisted activism with all his might, as he did anything that pulled him away from his work. For him, Transcendentalism was about universal ideas, timeless ideas. His interest in reform, as O.W. Firkins said, "was too far-reaching to be readily inflamed by specific causes." Yet when it came to the issue of slavery, to the mass displacement of Native Americans from their ancestral lands, Emerson could only use his pen for direct communication with the leaders involved. To not become an activist would have been as much a betrayal of his craft as if he had been on the wrong side of these issues.

Emerson would likely tell us that it was at the height of the Civil War that he most needed Confucius and Hindu philosophy and Sufi mysticism. It was then that he was especially drawn to powerful sources of wisdom. Wisdom he could then pour into his lectures and his writings for his audiences to hear. Of course he was aware that the most urgent subject on all of their minds was the rupture of their newborn nation. This was why it was important to lift his listeners to higher planes of thought.

Any American artist who was working on a project in September of 2001 can relate deeply with the conflict Emerson faced throughout his life. On September 11 we suddenly felt that our work was superfluous, that it mattered not one iota whether it was completed or not — unless it gave direct voice to the most urgent problems in the world, unless it addressed those problems in some meaningful way. At the time I was immersed in a novel about the dynamic dialogue between science and religion at the turn of the millennium. I had spent years in intensive research. When I turned on the news and saw the Twin Towers exploding, I felt what every American felt. What difference did it make what any of us was creating? Our world had essentially come to an end. After a while, like all Americans, I returned to my work, and even to the feeling that it was somehow important. And yet not a day has passed since when I have not felt the pull of "society vs. solitude."

I believe Emerson would tell us that one of the most important things we do as writers is to keep our ears attuned to what is happening in and *to* our world. "The scholar is a revealer of things," he said, "let him first learn the things. Let him not ... omit the work to be done." It is only by this effort that we develop the most valuable thing we have as writers — our own clear awareness of where we would steer the world if it were within our power to do so. Creative reading, then, includes not just reading that inspires us and moves us to new thought but also reading that gives us a clear picture of the world as it is.

What is the most important reason to become conscious, thoughtful observers of life? To develop our own views on the critical issues facing humanity? Because this is the most essential tilling we do as writers, the tilling within ourselves.

The idea that in order to become substantial writers we must become substantial people — this is a difficult thing to convey for anyone but the likes of Emerson, for anyone but a person who was described by those who knew him as a "beautiful transparent soul," a man who "lived in constant obedience to the demands of his higher nature," a man "whose being revolved on a center of integrity as a personal law unto itself." For the rest of us, talking about things like character and integrity and morality and virtue can only invite fierce personal scrutiny. And how would any of us fare? One of the books I read on writing was about this very subject, about how important it is for writers to be moral people and to promote morality through their writing. Halfway through the book when the author began naming some of his contemporaries and trashing them for not being moral enough, I had to put the book down.

Emerson did teach. He believed that teaching was the scholar's highest aim. He even believed that the creative writer should aspire to nothing less than "to supply the axis on which the frame of things turns." In order to do this, he said, "the iron must be of good quality." Emerson's iron, by all accounts, was of the highest quality. And yet he did not preach. As Chapman said, "His works are all one single attack on moral cowardice. But he assails it not by railings and scorn, but by positive and stimulating suggestion ... He managed through the power of suggestion, through "gleams and beams ... to urge his audiences to their own sense of right."

How did Emerson achieve the level of moral persuasion that inspired his reputation as a spiritual teacher, a sage? Every one of his biographers has arrived at the same conclusion. As John McAleer expressed it, "Emerson's eloquence in affirming that in building character men could lift the state of mankind was the best of his gifts ... And nothing persuaded men more of the feasibility of his message than the example of his own conduct." Oliver Wendell Holmes put it more succinctly: "What Emerson taught others to be, he was himself." And as Gay Wilson Allen summed it up, "Character pleads louder than art."

Emerson espoused ideas that marked him an "infidel" to many of his time. Others of his generation were ostracized and even imprisoned for defending the very thing Emerson stood for — the right to an individual lived experience of faith. And yet Emerson lived his entire life as a revered member of his community. He was embraced by diverse audiences everywhere he went and was sought out by artists and thinkers and scholars from far and wide. He was considered by many "the conscience of the nation." And as John Jay Chapman described it, "his figure could be seen from Europe towering like Atlas over the culture of the U.S." The very same man, Waldo Emerson, never claimed to be anything more than an "endless seeker." He referred to his own genius as "a poor sterile Yankeeism" that needed to be "tasked." He was a quiet thoughtful presence wherever he convened with others, whether at a Concord town meeting as an attentive observer or in a group of his intellectual peers. He was universally viewed as a man inseparable from his ideals, and as a noble, sincere and gracious human being.

Among the many things Emerson gave us is the opportunity to believe that the highest human qualities do matter. He even persuades us that true creative writing has less to do with the quality of the writing than it does with the quality of the writer.

When Emerson said, "a writer must live and die by his writing," he was talking about all that goes into making a writer a writer, as well as what makes writing a writer's life.

He was also stressing that whatever a writer is doing he is always writing. A scholar is a scholar all the time.

> The scholar studies in his sleep, in his waking, in his meals, in his pleasures ...

Which brings us to the most fundamental thing that writing requires, which I am mentioning last when it should have come first. It is something we rarely think about in relation to writing, though the demand for it is great. We need good health. We need it to keep our minds alert and to enable our bodies to sit for hours in a poised position with our eyes glued to our computer screens. We need it to be perched for days on end with books propped in our hands. We so underestimate how involved our bodies become in the act of writing. If we ignore them long enough we do pay a price. We have to take breaks and get out and walk! We have to give our eyes the opportunity for long-distance vision and rest. We have to *breathe* the way we breathe only when we are in motion.

Many writers find that regular walking not only gives them needed exercise, it also helps them get in touch with their deeper thoughts — the ones that linger in the recesses until we oxygenate them out. Emerson was famous for his walking. This was the way he fought against ill health all his life. And he did so with gusto. He not only walked in the woods daily, as his son Edward said, when he traveled to his lecture engagements, "he almost always refused offers to ride in a carriage ... He would walk across the city to his train, carrying his rather heavy leathern travelling bag in his hand at such a speed that a companion must run to keep up with him. 'When you have worn out your shoes,' he would say, 'the strength of the sole-leather has gone into the fibre of your body.'" There is no doubt that regular walking helped Emerson remain vigorous enough to be as prolific as he was. There is also no doubt that many an idea came to him while he was absorbing the strength from his shoe leather.

Is this what that man meant years ago when he told me how much work writing is? Was he talking about the energy it takes — to live full lives, and keep ourselves healthy, and spend long hours alone, and invest in deep relationships, and commune with Nature, and read voraciously, and work hard at becoming conscious human beings with our own worldview? That particular man would no doubt tell us, "Oh brother, you are just getting started." The work he was talking about was the work beyond the tilling. The actual dirt-under-the-fingernails *work* of writing.

As every gardener and farmer and grower-of-corn would tell us, the tilling of our plot of ground is just the beginning of the work and the care involved in growing something of our own. No matter how much tilling we may have done as writers, we must still face the hard work that goes into writing. And it is done the same way, each time, by each one of us — word by word.

Word by Word

As I said from the start, I have little to offer you on the subject of how to write — except perhaps to remind us both that every great author, every great work of writing began with the same question in mind. Pulling those first words out of ourselves and placing them one after the other, one sentence after the other — this is some of the hardest work we will ever do.

When we read a great book, one that holds us captive from the first word to the last, we cannot help feeling that it was planned from the start to be exactly what it is. We imagine that it flowed from the author in the very form it is in. And yet every written work represents a long and arduous journey — one with stops and starts and twists and turns, struggles and surprises, even major collisions — and one in which the author does not have her hands on all of the controls.

Why do I say that thinking about how to write only gets in the way of creative writing? Because we can't put our trust entirely in what comes to us from within if we are looking outside ourselves for guidance on anything. And that is what we are doing when we are thinking about how to write. We are looking outside ourselves.

In reality, there is no guidance to be given. Because no one knows how you write. They may know how they write. Or how they think great writers write. Or how they think all writers should write. But the only one who knows how you write is you. And you can only discover this through the process of writing. Once that first daunting question of "what to write" has been answered for you, "how to write" comes in the same way — with a life of its own.

If it sounds as though I am dismissing all of the wisdom that has been captured in books and courses on how to write — I am truly not. I believe every one of those authors would tell you that the advice they have to give will only be useful to you once you are writing, once you have taken that first leap and are writing what you feel called to write. Instruction in how to write is much like instruction in a computer program: It only makes sense when you are hands-on, when you are engaged in a project that is personal and meaningful to you. This is why we hear writing teachers say that they cannot teach anyone how to write, only how to re-write, that this is the only instruction in writing it is possible to give.

But don't we need to learn the principles of good writing before we can write? I agree entirely with Stephen King on this one: "One either absorbs the grammatical principles of one's native language in conversation and in reading or one does not." This is the way any of us learns how to use our language, through reading and conversation, through reading and listening. The more we do of these two things, the more we develop our own command of language, our own comfort with language, and our own way of expressing our self.

Some would hear this as anti-education. Yet Stephen King and I are both pro-education. What we are saying is that the most effective education for all of us is the one going on inside us all the time, the one that began when we were children and started following our instincts about the things that interested us, started paying close attention to everything that would educate us in those very inclinations. As aspiring writers, every bit of reading and communicating we do is part of our training as writers.

When I first committed to writing, though it is true I did not look for guidance from books or teachers, I was still looking outside myself. I struggled every day with the question of "how to write." If I were to choose one thing that I wish could have been impressed upon me then, it would be this:

Writing is a *relationship*. A relationship with ourselves, with ideas, with language, with the creative process. Like every other relationship, we learn by throwing ourselves into it and following our instincts. We learn by relating. The best lessons we learn about relationships we learn *in* relationships. And we learn the most when we risk the most of ourselves. Yes, we can look for wisdom and counsel from outside the relationship. But don't we only do this when we feel we need help? When we feel we might improve our relationship by understanding some of the guiding principles that have been helpful to others? If we don't just jump in and pursue our own natural instincts, we miss out on all of the discovery involved. It is the discovery and the learning and growing that makes writing such a rich experience.

This is a small example but it may be a good one to explain what I mean: If we read in a book on how to write, as I recently did, that one of the techniques we should employ in our writing is to vary the length of our sentences in order to create rhythm for the reader — and we follow that advice — we deprive ourselves of that wonderful moment when we *experience* rhythm in our writing, rhythm that naturally appeared out of our own honest expression. We deprive ourselves of the pleasure of recognizing it and examining it and understanding how it came about. If we come at it from the other direction, deliberately varying our sentences, this can only impede our honest expression.

A more potent example might be in relation to that cardinal rule of "expelling every superfluous word." If we write with this rule in mind, anticipating every word that might be stricken by a teacher or an editor, we deny ourselves everything there is to discover about our own natural expression, our own way of relating with a reader. This accepted rule of writing is important for one reason. It is about the reader's ease in getting at what we are saying. Instead of thinking about the rule, or any rule, it helps if we concentrate solely on our relationship with the reader, the one we imagine to be most interested in what we have to say. When we talk with an old friend, for instance, one we haven't spoken with in a long time, we don't talk about anything superfluous. We go straight to the heart of what we most need to share. We talk about the important things that are happening in each of our lives and about the feelings we share only with our closest friends. Readers are like those old friends on the phone with whom we have precious limited time. What matters is not how many words we use but that we have an authentic connection.

John Casey, in his *Beyond the First Draft: The Art of Fiction*, tells a story that perfectly demonstrates this point — that it is not about how many words we use but about choosing the right words. Casey says that after both his agent and his editor told him his 604-page novel was too long — and he did some rewriting and sent it back as a 640-page novel — they both told him separately, "Good. It's much shorter." When a piece of writing works, when it holds the interest of the reader, no one cares how long it is. They especially do not care if the author used some unnecessary words.

I cannot resist expressing my own thoughts on this particular rule, which caused me a bit of angst as well during my early years of writing. When we are trying to get comfortable with our own way of expressing our self, the constant concern about economy of language can have a strangling effect. Today, though I am sure I would be accused of using too many words at times, I no longer have anyone else's hatchet in mind as I "amputate, amputate," as Emerson put it. I do constantly pare down and simplify my language, but only according to my own sensibilities.

The truth is, to my sensibilities, something has been lost in the thinning of literature that has occurred over the years, especially in contrast to the days of Emerson and Thoreau and Hawthorne and Whitman, a time when literature was both deeply textured and deeply felt. If we are all supposed to write like Hemingway now and are constantly concerned with expelling superfluous words — well, it seems we are not only telling young writers how to write, we are telling them that the thinning of literature is something to be valued. Who knows what Hawthorne or Melville or Dickens or George Eliot might be out there somewhere!

Yes, there are rules of good writing that are important for every writer to know. They are helpful in making us better writers. But if we look to those rules to guide us in our approach to writing, if we concentrate on the rules and tools and techniques, we will be writing someone else's idea of what we should write rather than our own.

And aren't creative writers exempt from rules anyway? Isn't that what being creative is about — breaking rules and being original and creating new forms? As I asked myself this question and let it roll around in my head for a while, the answer again came from Emerson.

When Emerson said, "The scholar is bound to stand for all the virtues and all the liberties," he was of course talking about something far more important than how we should write. He was talking about what we should aspire to achieve through our writing. And yet if we apply this same principle to our responsibility *to* writing, we find some interesting insight about writing too.

There is no greater *virtue* in the art of writing than our commitment to honor our language, to strive in every way we can to write as well as we can. Truly great writing, writing that stands the test of time, is not just writing that conveys what it set out to convey, it also stands as a monument to the art of writing. If anything worth doing is worth doing well, then attempting "world-making" verse deserves the whole of us. It deserves everything we have to give.

At the same time, there is no *liberty* more worth defending than the liberties taken by the creative artist, the liberties she sometimes takes as she creates forms that do not always allow her to comply with the rules. In writing, there are times we break the rules out of ignorance or neglect. But there are also times we break them knowingly, because no matter how hard we may work — at adjusting a sentence, for instance, to make it correct, we find in the end we must leave it exactly as it came to us. We see that though it may be technically incorrect, it expresses precisely what we mean to express.

We have all had the experience of reading a book and suddenly stopping because of a difficult sentence. We have to go back and read it again because it is ambiguous or grammatically awkward or somehow confusing. There is probably not a single author who has not at some time neglected to fix a bad sentence. We find them in even our most treasured books — almost as though they are there to remind us that even great authors make mistakes. There are also times when we recognize that a sentence is incorrect and yet we feel the author has conveyed exactly what was intended. We even find it hard to imagine that the thought could have been better expressed in any other way. These are the kinds of liberties writers sometimes take even when we are committed to honoring our language.

What language has taught me over the years is that it too has a life of its own, one that is every bit deserving of a real relationship. If we think of it as a lifeless set of rules and tools and techniques, we miss out entirely on that relationship. As Emerson said, "Every writer is a skater and must go partly where he would and partly where the skates carry him." As writers we come to recognize our language as one of the forces at play on the ice with us. If we approach it with respect and even humility, we discover that it is tireless in its openness and receptivity. It yields to us and engages with us in our own exploration and discovery.

I could fill a hundred pages here with the fascinating things that have happened in my own evolving relationship with language — my own unique exploration of the power of words and the "architectonics" of writing. (What a great word!) I will share one, which I believe is a good one for showing how intimate we become with every nuance of language. So intimate, we even develop our own relationship with punctuation — something that in the beginning can seem such a minor consideration. Over time we see that even punctuation has a dynamism of its own, one that never ceases to engage us in internal deliberations.

In my case, I have had the most interesting relationship with the comma. Yes, that seemingly insignificant little black mark that we use to separate words and phrases. When I began writing I used the comma a great deal. Far too often, my friend Connie insisted. I placed it wherever I felt the need to emphasize a thought. And because I am an emotional writer — I write about things I am passionate about — I emphasized a lot.

My dear friend Connie Dunlap has also been one of my treasured first readers since I began writing years ago. Connie spent her career as director of libraries at major universities and among her many affinities for the written word is her expertise as a grammarian. Whenever I share my work with her, in addition to giving me her overall response, she assesses for me, as no one else could I'm convinced, the *readability* of what I have written. She also goes through at my urging and takes a red pen to anything that is an assault on good grammar. The one thing that came up repeatedly, especially during our early years, was my incessant use of commas.

Connie and I have enjoyed great fun over the years with our comma tug-of-war, to the point of referring to her as the "CEO of the Comma Savings and Loan." "I don't know why I even bother to point this one out," she would say, "You're just going to leave it in anyway." She knows me well enough to know that in the end I go with my gut on things, even at the expense of being incorrect. She also knows that every comma she points to is likely to have been put in and put out a hundred times before she sees it on the page.

Connie has made me a better writer, first because of her friendship, which has been one of the most cherished of my lifetime — and also because of her keen eye and thorough knowledge of the proper use of language. She has also made me a better writer by calling my attention to the power of a single comma. She has sensitized me to the use of commas both in my reading and my writing. As a result I have come to see that unnecessary commas, commas used only for emphasis, can interrupt the fluidity that is so important to the reader. Today my work is far less riddled with commas. I even cite Emerson wishing I could remove some of those little marks that, truly, just get in the way.

There are of course people with different and equally valid opinions on the proper use of punctuation. What matters is that we ask for input from people we respect and that we give care and attention to every single decision, even if it means putting punctuation in and out a hundred times until we feel it is right.

I share this example of course because of the pleasure it gives me and the pleasure I hope it will give my friend Connie to read about it here. (You comma Gestapo, you.) But also because it illustrates how involved we become with language. As we write and rewrite and rewrite and rewrite, we develop a real relationship with language, one that we come to recognize is our very own. We also recognize that, just as with any relationship, it is made rich by how much we invest in it, by how much we give of ourselves.

How does the musician learn to play her instrument and compose her own music? She plays a lot of notes. She makes a lot of music. How does the painter learn to transfer her vision to the canvas? She dips her brush in a lot of paint and paints and paints and paints. Like every other art form, writing takes time. It takes *practice* — there is no other word to use. There is no possible route around the fact that good writing is the product of long, hard labor — or that becoming a good writer takes years.

If we had the opportunity to survey every great writer on the subject of how to write, I believe that to a person they would tell us that finding one's own way as a writer is what makes a writer a writer. They would also say that they think too much of writing to ever reduce it to "how to's." Yes, they might offer some practical advice as they continued to ruminate on their own relationship with writing. But they would also emphasize how deeply personal a relationship it is, one that never ceases to fascinate.

Stephen King, in the foreword to his book *On Writing*, declared, "Most books about writing are filled with bullshit." This is a delightfully unvarnished way of saying that a lot of what is out there on the subject may well only hold you back or get in your way. He also freely admits, as other writers have, that in truth writers don't really understand a whole lot about their own processes. As Nadine Gordimer expressed it, "To analyze it would be to look down while crossing a canyon on a tightrope."

No matter who we are, no matter how experienced we are at writing, we never stop wrestling with the question of "how to write." We confront it with each new project and each new page and each new blank space on the page. But the truth is that what we are really wrestling with has little to do with anything that happens between us and the page. It is what happens in the other direction, within us, that is the real work of writing. The "how to" we most need to focus on is how to trust what we find there, how to own what is ours to write. This is the real work of learning how to write.

"The Soul's Emphasis is Always Right"

*"By putting the ear close to the soul,
learn always the true way."*

For most of my life I had thought of Emerson as a reliable source of spiritual inspiration. When I turned to him with creative writing in mind I was amazed at the force with which his spirit took over this process and elevated it to brand new heights. At one point I even wondered if I was laying too much emphasis here on his spiritual ideas, if the reader might find this a diversion from the real subject at hand. And then it came to me that seeking guidance as spiritual beings and seeking guidance as creative writers are two inseparable things. Emerson would say they are one and the same.

If you are truly driven to creative writing, you no doubt agree. You probably also recognize your soul as the essence of who you are, as the part of you that is the true source of everything you have to give.

Emerson believed that every great thinker and writer was speaking from the depth of his soul. He attributed their greatness, their genius, to their trust in what they found there, to the access they were given to universal truths. What is this instinct that he believed is at the core of the human soul? Why did he believe so strongly that when we trust in it completely we do the work that is ours to do, the work "by which nature contrives to get the work of the world done."

In order to fully appreciate Emerson's views on the power within the soul, it helps to look at how he arrived at them, how he came to trust in his own soul.

Emerson inherited his understanding of the soul the same way most of us do, through his family's religious tradition. As a boy he was taught the Puritan Christian doctrine of the soul. When he reached his point of crisis with his faith — his conflict with institutions of faith — he opened himself up to every available avenue of spiritual inspiration. He also faced the stark reality that no belief system holds the answers to unanswerable questions. He even embraced the idea that true "knowledge is the knowing that we cannot know." He arrived at the conclusion that it is the questioning that is important, especially for a person of faith. It is the constant search for truth that is the highest reverence we can pay to the ultimate unknowable, the power behind the universe.

Emerson was so committed to questioning he even opened his mind to doubt. He listened intently to the arguments for atheism that were capably presented to him by his friend, Achille Murat, the "noble soul" with whom he spent days aboard ship in a feverish exchange of ideas. Of Murat, he wrote, "He is a philosopher, a scholar ... with a mind surpassing mine in the variety of its research ... I love and honor this intrepid doubter. He possesses as ardent a love of truth as that which animates me."

It was after Emerson had freed himself from all religious constraints and even entertained the notion of doubt that he learned the true depth of his own faith. He experienced it in his own soul. He knew as he could only know after rigorous questioning that his faith in God was "indestructible." "I have known that I existed directly from God," he said. He had received this truth directly, not from any vision or voice — he did not believe in such things — he had felt it in his own being. It was his own *lived* experience of faith that convinced him that "internal evidence outweighs all others" and that "belief consists in accepting the affirmations of the soul; unbelief in denying them." And so began his lifelong quest to understand and to advocate for the human soul.

Emerson came to view the instinct at the core of the soul as the soul's own deep intuition. It was the part of us that is inseparably connected with the ultimate "perceiver and revealer of truth." He believed that each individual, without any guidance from any institution, could find in his own soul, not just a powerful faith in God and an "original relation to the universe," but his most infallible guide for how to live his life.

For the rest of his life Emerson not only relied on this inner instinct as the true source of faith — it was his unflinching reliance on this same inner guide that was also the source of his character. And as even his staunchest critics recognized, his character and his genius were one and the same. His genius, he would tell us, was the genius that is found at the core of each human soul.

Emerson's great faith in the soul, in addition to being criticized on theological grounds, has also been viewed by many as naïve. To believe that all people possess an inner instinct, an infallible guide that will lead them in the right direction — what planet was he living on? One of the strongest objections to Emerson has been that his idealism, his romanticism, blinded him to the dark side of human nature, that he did not acknowledge the power of evil in the world. But Emerson was too brilliant and lived too full a life not to be keenly aware of the darkest tendencies in human nature. One of his most deeply held beliefs in fact was his faith in the compensatory justice that is being rendered all the time, for every act of good, every act of evil.

O.W. Firkins brought this matter into the clearest focus for me when he said, "Emerson was perhaps the most sweeping, the most fearless, the most insistent idealist that ever lived." On the charge that he was oblivious to the realities of evil, he said, "It would be more exact to say he overrated the *preponderance* of good." This is perhaps the most succinct description of Emerson's core belief — his unyielding faith in the preponderance of good.

As his son Edward explained, Emerson believed that when a man comes to know his own soul, "lower beliefs were sure to give way by displacement when higher ones were given." He believed that if a man is ruled by evil inclinations it is because "there is so much of his nature which is unlawfully withholden from him." What did Emerson believe was unlawfully withholden from the man who chooses evil over good? Richard Geldard answered this question brilliantly and succinctly in *God in Concord: Ralph Waldo Emerson's Awakening to the Infinite*: "The individual would take the moral path, given the gift of reflective thought."

This is what self-reliance is about. It is about self-reflection, contemplation, an inner life of reflective thought. Emerson was convinced that when we engage in true self-reliance, when we consult our innermost soul, we cannot deny what we find there. We cannot betray it. This is why he said, "I cannot find language of sufficient energy to convey my sense of the sacredness of private integrity." He believed that if every human being were to rely on his or her own soul, our collective souls would lead the world in the right direction.

Here we come to the heart of the "Emersonian" in "Emersonian creative writing." Emerson believed that when the creative writer relies entirely on his own soul, he will always be guided in the right direction, the direction of Good.

Emerson spent much of his life contemplating the qualities that were present in all great men. He looked to Plato and Montaigne and Goethe and other *Representative Men*, thinkers and writers who achieved a "sublime reliance on the simple force of Truth." He arrived at some important conclusions: Great men are *affirmative*. "The soul looks steadily forward." "Genius looks forward." "Genius is the activity that repairs the decay of things." Why were the minds nearest the stars always affirmative, always pointing forward? Because by relying on what came to them through their own souls they became aligned with the deepest forces of the universe.

> All things proceed out of the same spirit, and all things conspire with it. Whilst a man seeks good ends, he is strong by the whole strength of nature.

> The highest and truest utterances of the poet are not his ... The poet knows he did not make his thought. No, his thoughts made him and made the sun and the stars.

It is impossible to separate Emerson's understanding of creativity from his understanding of Creation, which to Emerson was an ever-present, ongoing process. The entire universe, he believed, is driven by forces that are ever-renewing, ever forward, bent on achieving their highest nature and ever-progressing toward that aim.

> A breath of will blows eternally through the universe of souls in the direction of the Right and Necessary ... All loss, all pain is particular, the universe as a whole remains to the heart unhurt.

All nature is the rapid efflux of goodness executing and organizing itself.

This was the power that Emerson believed the creative artist is able to tap into, the same force that permeates and drives all of life. True creativity, he believed, is the ongoing work of Creation. And it is as accessible within each of us as it is within the life of the universe.

Creative writing, in Emerson's view, is writing that nourishes men's spirits and feeds their souls. It "cheers, raises and guides men" by throwing a light on the highest human qualities and deepest capacities. Yes, the creative writer may well take his readers into the darkest recesses of human experience. But never without a light to show the way out, to point to a higher direction. Above all, the creative writer is a bringer of hope.

In a perfect world, would there be any need for creative writing? Would any of us feel the need to create? These are questions that could engage the finest minds for a good long time. Perhaps in the final analysis they would all agree that the urge to create, the urge to engage in the creative process, to produce and appreciate beauty, to inspire and to move our fellow human beings — these are all important aspects of our humanness. And yet if there were no need to repair the decay of things, to point to a higher direction, would creativity not lack much of the urgency that drives it?

One of the other books on writing that I read in one sitting was Madeleine L'Engle's *Walking on Water: Reflections on Faith and Art*. In this case it was not so much a matter of being enthralled as it was of being provoked. And provoked I was to the very last page. Afterward, I was disappointed to learn Ms. L'Engle had died a few years earlier. I would have loved to have communicated with her about her book and feel sure we would have had some rich conversation. Among the things I would have told her is that I saw myself provoked in the same way Emerson was provoked by Swedenborg, the Christian mystic he was captivated by at the same time he was repelled by the limits he put on his own faith. I would tell her that reading her book I even found myself invoking Emerson's impassioned appeal — "Believe in magnetism, not in needles!"

Though I could never endorse Ms. L'Engle's idea that the sentiment is the exclusive domain of any religion, I did appreciate her important statement: "An artist cannot rest as long as there is suffering in the world." I feel sure she would have agreed that what we all hope for is to some day replace the word "artist" with "human being." Then we would have achieved our highest religion.

I do believe that people who are infected with a burning desire to create tend to also be people who are deeply affected by the suffering in the world, who wish with all their might that the elimination of suffering could be our highest human priority. They also tend to be people who feel they are not personally doing enough to assist their fellow beings, to actively work against injustice and suffering. They are even likely to struggle with these feelings all their lives in their own "society vs. solitude" battle.

What Emerson gave us, both through his direct urgings and in the knowledge of what his own works have achieved, is the absolute assurance that the creative writer *is* actively working to make a better world. She is engaged in a powerful force for change. We would have justification for believing this even in the knowledge of Emerson's influence on Thoreau, the young man in the audience the day he delivered "The American Scholar" who became his friend and protégé and grew into an outspoken abolitionist and activist and the author of

Walden, Civil Disobedience, and *Life Without Principle.* We would have it in the knowledge of the profound impact Emerson and Thoreau had on Gandhi and on Martin Luther King, and in Jane Addams' declaration that it was Emerson who inspired her to devote her life to crucial social reforms. Scholars continue to uncover compelling examples of how Emerson and Thoreau have inspired others to actively work for a better world.

None of us is naïve enough to believe that any one artist or writer can truly move the world in a higher direction. What is important is that we hold this intention at the heart of every effort we make — and that we hold fast to the Emersonian belief that "no ray of light, no pulse of good, is ever lost."

At this point in my life, I think of creative writing, and all art, in terms of that fundamental energy that we now know is the makings of everything. Every one of us, everything we touch, everything that appears to be nothing at all — it is all energy. And some of that energy has a value attached to it that is more powerful than we know. Every time we love someone, or create music, or plant a garden — every time we engage in a creative process — we are creating the kind of energy that offsets the negative forces in the world. Without it, the violence and the fear and suffering would be too much to bear. It would be too much for the world to bear. So when we throw ourselves into our art, when we work hard at creating, we are actually keeping the world's energy in balance. We are keeping the world alive.

This is the way Emerson viewed creative writing. It is the work that repairs the decay of things, that keeps the world alive and moving forward. In order to achieve this, he insisted, we need only ask to be a worthy instrument.

Relying entirely on ourselves, trusting in the voice that comes to us from within — this is a difficult thing for any of us to do. It is an even greater leap to reach beyond ourselves in an act of faith in powers greater than our own. And yet this is what true self-reliance is. It is a surrender to the force that is the very life in us, the force that drives all of the life around us — however unknowable we might recognize that force to be.

How in the world do we know when we are in touch with this force? When we are aligned with the deepest instincts of our soul? I believe Emerson would tell us the same thing he said about truth: "We know it as we know when we are awake that we are awake."

The "Idealism," the "Transcendentalism" to which Emerson subscribed was to Emerson a matter of living the life of the soul, of trusting the soul to guide us on our truest path. Nothing should deter us, he said. Nothing should divert us from this "all-containing virtue which we vainly dodge and postpone, but which must be met and obeyed at last, if we wish to be substance, and not accidents."

Most of us, most of the time, do not have the vision Emerson had. The things we see most clearly are the everyday demands of material existence — and the illusion that this is all that is. This is the real divide Ralph Waldo Emerson marked. The struggle we all face every day. The struggle between giving ourselves over to the world of "appearances," and devoting ourselves to our true life, the life within.

All of our world religions, all of our belief systems tell us that the soul is the most vital part of us, the only immortal part of us. Strip away all religious beliefs, we are still left with a fundamental view of the soul as our most defining essence, as the part of us that makes us who we are. And yet how often do we focus on the life of our soul? How often do we give it our full attention? Mr. Emerson would tell us that it is only after we have committed ourselves to our own inner life that we can become creative writers.

Aim High

"Lift your aims!" "Always do what you are afraid to do!" "Be generous and great and you will confer benefits on society!" These are things Emerson heard throughout his youth from his Aunt Mary. Emerson did aim high. So high he could only come to know the "innavigable sea of silent waves between us and the things we aim at." His aim was to open minds, to provoke thought, to awaken souls. His message was one of passionate reverence for the great sanctity of life, for the absolute connectedness and oneness of the universe, for the forwardness of all of life, for the eternal life of the soul.

How can any of us look to Emerson as a model for our own creative writing? How could we ever lift our aims so high? Emerson would tell us that the moment we were infected with the yearning to create, our aims were lifted for us.

Clearly, I have been an Emerson devotee all my adult life. Who can forget the first person who opened the gates for them to the life of the mind, who not only escorted them through but held them on their shoulders so they could have the highest possible view? At the same time, my devotion to Emerson, my euphoria throughout this process, has been for something far more significant than a single man. The truth is I am not quite able to wrap my mind around Emerson the man. I have viewed him now through the eyes of many different scholars and have been riveted by all I have learned. And yet Emerson the man, Emerson the real human being, remains an enigma to me. Perhaps this is the nature of true genius whenever it takes up residence in any human being.

Emerson ensured that the only way we would ever truly know him was through his written works. He did this in part by the power of the ideas he delivered like missiles. But also through the intensity of purpose with which he lived his life. He provided no distractions, no significant failings, no contradictions where contradictions matter most. The only way he stood out in his personal life was in the quality of his being.

What Emerson was in my view was a *carrier*. A carrier in an irreplaceable line of carriers that have passed ideas along through the centuries. As he continually reminds us, he introduced no new ideas. "Every book is a quotation," he said. "No great men are original." He said this of Plato and of all the minds he recognized as nearest the stars. "The power which they communicate is not theirs," he said, "When we are exalted by ideas, we do not owe this to Plato, but to the idea, to which, also, Plato was debtor ... The greatest genius is the most indebted man."

Emerson's genius was in capturing ideas and molding them and shaping them into new forms. His genius was in the synthesis, in the molding and shaping, and in his extraordinary forms. As Stephen Whicher said, he was at times able to achieve "an incandescence not quite like anything else in literature." An incandescence that reflected his highest genius — his passion for ideas and his gift for evoking the same passion in others.

What Emerson could not have understood during his lifetime was that he too was one of the minds nearest the stars. He was not only a carrier of truths that had been recognized by others before him; he was also an anticipator of ideas far advanced of his time. Was Emerson's generation ready to hear that the universe is driven by forces that are relentlessly pursuing a higher direction, a more perfect unity, a more balanced whole? That human life is spirit become conscious of itself? That human beings are part of a universal plan, both individually and collectively, and that by becoming one with Nature we become one with our highest selves? Are we ready to absorb such ideas today?

Emerson was also a carrier of something else, something many authors have attempted to describe — and always in the same luminous language. Whitman described it as "an indefinable something which flows out and over you like a flood of light." He was talking about the transcendent energy that flows out of Emerson's works and into readers, inspiring them to also become creative writers.

Yes, I too have felt this "indefinable something" which has been recognized by so many as uniquely Emersonian. And I reverently put forward the term "Emersonian creative writing" to describe the kind of writing Emerson achieved, the kind to which he would have each of us aspire. But here is the ultimate irony in Emerson: To be Emersonian is not to be Emersonian. It is to shake off the need to be a follower of anyone. To be Emersonian is to strive to achieve a pure reliance on one's own soul.

As Walt Whitman said, "The best part of Emersonianism is, it breeds the giant that destroys itself. No teacher ever taught that has so provided for his pupil's setting up independently." And as Lawrence Buell followed, "He even invites you to kill him off," which makes him "one of the most unusual authority figures in the history of western culture."

Emerson said that the use of great men is "to reveal us to ourselves ... to learn the deepest secret of our capacity." What Emerson reveals to us is our highest selves. He calls our attention to our own untouched, unimagined resources, the power that resides *within*. He also continually reminds us that universal truths belong to all of us, that they were ours "from eternity." When we are overcome by the wisdom and eloquence of a great thinker, he asks us, "Were not the words that ... brought the blood to your cheeks, that made you tremble or delighted you ... Was this not truth you knew before?"

It is not surprising that Emerson's most enthusiastic audience was the youth of his time. Young people, budding artists and scholars, flocked to Emerson and were galvanized by his ideas. What young person does not want to hear that they should not tie their fresh lives to a dead past, that they should trust in their own souls and live authentic lives and remake the world into a better place? The purest idealism always finds its natural home in the young.

I confess that throughout this process I have imagined my ideal reader to be a young person. In fact, it has become increasingly clear that what I have been writing is the book I wish I could have read when I was twenty years old. If you are still with me at this point and you are not a young person, for what it's worth, I am convinced that what we bring to creative writing later in life can be even more valuable than the idealism of youth. We can come to it with a seasoned soul. A soul that *chooses* idealism, even knowing full well the costs. (As Emerson said, "the soul *becomes*.")

Whatever your age, if you are truly driven to creative writing, I am convinced you will find in Emerson everything you need. Somehow he manages to make us believers in our own "unattained but attainable self." He manages to convince us that each and every one of us is "a new and incalculable power" — and that that which is ours to express is brand new in the life of the universe.

What is the relevance of Emerson today? In today's vast, multicultural America? A nineteenth century white male New Englander who enjoyed the privileges of the cultured elite? A man who used the word "man" whenever he spoke of human beings? Emerson was a creative writer at a time when there was no such thing as "media" of any kind, when even libraries and daily newspapers were a distant dream for the vast majority of Americans. The primary source of education for ninety-five percent of the population was the series of invited speakers who came to the local lyceum or community gathering place. Many of the orators were trained as preachers and much of the oratory was preaching. (Emerson's oratory, Emerson's life work, was more of a prayer. It was "the contemplation of the facts of life from the highest point of view.")

The important thing to remember about Emerson is that none of the features of his own life, or his life in relation to other lives, could possibly have escaped his examination. And though he was certainly a product of his own life and time — and even a devout patriot, as invested as any in the American ideals he helped to define — Emerson's concern was not for any particular society, it was for humankind. Most important, he viewed all of earthly life as a mere stopping-off point in the life of the soul.

As for the assault on our twenty-first century ears, hearing the word "man" used so exclusively — as a woman, I must say this: Emerson said two important things about women as far as I'm concerned. And one of them said it all for me — "Women see better than men." He believed that all genius has a feminine element within it, and that

"Woman is the power of civilization." The other statement he made was on the subject of whether women should be given the right to vote, which he was asked at a time when such ideas were just a glimmer in the minds of the most progressive few. He said, "Certainly all my points would be sooner carried in the state if women voted." Emerson may have been a nineteenth century male but he was as harnessed to his century as the women in his life were. Women like Mary Moody Emerson and Margaret Fuller, Madame de Stael, George Sand, George Eliot — women whose voices would carry through centuries. Today, Emerson would use different words than "man." And he would use the female at every opportunity. He would say it is up to men to actively root out sexism, just as it is up to whites to root out racism.

In asking about Emerson's relevance in today's world, there are far more important questions at stake than whether Emerson's language and style grow increasingly remote. (One even wonders if he deliberately adopted a style that also could not be harnessed to his or to any era.) The far more important questions have to do, not with Emerson, but with us. If Emerson's vision was for a world in which the life of the soul is valued above any of the illusions of material existence, we have to ask — Is the material any less primary today than it was in Emerson's time? Or has humankind, with America in the lead, taken "materialism" to brand new heights?

Perhaps the real question about Emerson's relevance is the same as it was in Emerson's day — What is his relevance in the "real" world? The world in which we live. One thing is for certain, for those who perceive the world in which we live as the only reality, Emerson will have little relevance in any time. For those who believe that true reality lies in a higher realm, a realm of which our earthly life is only a glimpse, Emerson is as relevant today as he was to the Transcendentalists of nineteenth century New England. For the aspiring creative writer — he is as relevant as any writer you will read.

Does Emerson continue to be read and to inspire thought? We can only hope the answer to this question reveals as much about us as it does about Emerson. As Joel Myerson reported in his 2000 *Historical Guide to Ralph Waldo Emerson*, "in the last decade alone, nearly one thousand articles and books have been published discussing this life, ideas, and writings." According to Joel Porte, "Emerson will continue to appeal to those Americans who know where to look for their truth-speakers ... The fortunes of the author will thus keep pace with the fortunes of the republic. In this sense, Emerson's reputation is, and will remain, a measure of our own stature." And Ronald Bosco asserts that the day we stop reading this "principal architect of American culture" — stop thinking about and writing about Ralph Waldo Emerson — "that part of America he created will cease to exist."

Jacob Needleman, in *The Spiritual Emerson*, goes even further in his assessment of Emerson's importance, not just for Americans but for the human race. He says, "The life of our world may now depend on grasping, really grasping ... what this nineteenth century thinker had to tell us ... Emerson can awaken us from ... the spell of sullen illusions ... about what human beings are and what they can become: illusions that deny the true metaphysical nobility of man."

Was it Emerson's aim to lead humankind in a higher direction? Did he imagine his beloved America becoming the symbol of hope he envisioned for the world? Emerson was an idealist, but an idealist with his feet firmly planted on the ground. As O. W. Firkins said, "He was a man built to exert a rare influence upon a certain kind of highly sensitive and clarified human material." His highest aim was the one he achieves with every aspiring writer who feels that flood of light flowing out of his works and into them. His hope was to inspire us to lift our aims as high as the sky.

> All literature is yet to be written ... Religion is yet to be settled on its fast foundations in the breast of man; and politics, and philosophy, and letters, and art ... Poetry has scarce chanted its first song ...

> What Plato has thought *you* may think, what a saint has felt *you* may feel, what at any time has befallen any man *you* can understand ... Build therefore your own world!

The Process is the Prize

What is it about writing that holds such allure for so many of us? That drives some of us to great lengths, even to great costs, just to be able to pursue it? I believe each of us somewhere in our deepest heart believes we have something to say, something that is uniquely ours to give to the world. We know this instinctively because we know that no matter who we are, no matter what kind of life we have lived, we hold something of value in our own experience and in what we have learned from it. This, I believe, is what the drive to write is about. It is about discovering what is ours to give.

For those of us who are fascinated by the search for truth, by the quest for meaning and purpose in life, the desire to write is inescapable. After all, the truths we have found, the truths that have reverberated inside us, we have for the most part found in books, in the ideas expressed by the thinkers and writers who have inspired us. How could we not begin to dream that we too might make a life for ourselves in the world of ideas?

As for the notion that writers are driven by a desire to make some kind of mark on the world, to leave something behind us that will give significance to our life — I personally find it hard to believe that a single writer ever wrote with this thought in mind. We humans are driven by far more short-sighted needs and impulses. We do what we do to improve the quality of our immediate lives, to make them as rich as they can be. Even the impulse to contribute to the world is one that enriches us. It fills us with a sense of hope. And hope is something we all need.

The fact is that few writers leave an indelible mark on the world. But we all leave indelible marks on the hearts of others. And this in the end is what art is about. It is about touching the humanness in one another and reminding one another that we are all in this life together and we all carry the same feelings inside us. What matters in the end is not how many people we touch but how we touch the ones we do.

I have just devoted an entire book to the Emersonian idea that we should reach for the sky with our writing. We should aspire to be carriers of universal ideas and to influence the making of a better world. So how can that possibly square with saying that it is okay that most of us will never achieve that? That it doesn't really matter how much our works are even read? Because the greatest rewards that come from creative writing come not from any end result but from the process itself.

We hear all the time from artists in every field that it is the work itself that motivates the artist. It is not the prospect of money or fame, or even of completing a particular project. It is the *process* that is the real prize. This book will have little value if I stop at saying this again. So I am going to be very specific about the rewards that can come to even the most unsuccessful writer, the writer whose only reward is in the process itself. If I have any expertise at all, this would certainly be it. And the truth is, I believe with all my heart that even if I were a highly successful writer, this would be the thing most worth sharing.

The first major gift that comes to us through the process of writing is the opportunity to learn. And not in the way we learn in school or in any kind of instruction or training — unless we are fortunate enough to learn on a subject that brings us to life in a way nothing else can. The kind of learning creative writing inspires is learning that excites us, that activates our intellect and awakens our passion for knowledge and insight. It also fills us with a sublime sense of freedom, because our sole objective is to satisfy ourselves, not to meet standards or measures defined or imposed by anyone else.

As Emerson said, we can only find that spark of genius inside us if we are searching amongst the flames, if we write about subjects that create a fire in us. Once we have experienced that moment of "illumination," once we know what it is that we need to write, we naturally pursue our own creative learning. The kind of learning Emerson called his "second education." For him this was the books he hid below his desk all through elementary school and that he pored over in his "chamber alone," which he said was the only thing of value he found at college.

Emerson was critical of educational institutions for the same reason he criticized religious ones — he recognized how important they were and how much more they could be doing. Today, I am convinced he would stand in awe of many of the scholars America has produced, as well as the institutions that support them. He would recognize in many professional scholars the same fervor and creativity that drives the artist. Yet he would also agree with the ones who assert that our system of education continues to fall short on its primary mission, which is to "set the minds of the youth on flame."

When we become engaged in creative writing we understand how Emerson came to speak of "creative reading" and "creative writing" in the same breath, how he came to view the life of the soul and the life of the mind as one thing. We cannot commit to creative writing without becoming passionate about learning.

This of course includes the reading and research we do for particular projects — which can be so significant I have found myself remarking to friends, "Writing is eighty percent input and twenty percent output!" The research alone can be some of the most exciting learning we have ever done. But when the real magic comes in is when we find ourselves learning from everything around us the entire time we are writing. Everything that is said to us, every event we experience, every film we see, has some new insight to offer us. It is as though all of the life around us is participating in our creative processing.

I must share another Emerson story which I hope will make what I just said sound a little less crazy. One of the interesting things I noticed about Emerson was the consistent presence of pears in his life. In each biography I read there was some new mention of pears. When he was a boy, for instance, his family lived next door to a judge who had a pear tree in his yard. Pears were of course a delicacy in a family supported by a minister's salary. When the neighbor's tree was heavy with pears Waldo would hang on the fence and relish the thought of the forbidden fruit that was out of his reach in every way. Later, at Harvard, when he worked as a student assistant to the president, whenever the president rewarded a student he would give him pears — something Waldo witnessed many times, though there was no mention of his ever partaking of them himself. After he had settled in Concord, he built an orchard on his property — some say as many as a hundred trees, most of which were pear. He would sometimes reward himself after long hours of work by standing at the window of his study and savoring a ripe pear. And in his later years while visiting Egypt, when he was introduced to mandarin oranges, he enjoyed them so much he could only compare them to pears.

As I came to view pears as a symbol in Emerson's life, it was particularly interesting to read his son Edward's account of what his father *learned* from his pear trees. As he said, they gave him much more than the fruit they produced. He learned that by "taking seedlings in a 'state of amelioration' and by successive plantings of the first seeds of the best, in five or six generations would bear superior fruit ... Here, as everywhere, Mr. Emerson found new evidence that barriers and limitations were not really but only seemingly fixed; that rightly aimed effort could break them down." No writer could read that insight Emerson shared with his son and not recognize its full impact in Emerson's mind. The writer learns from everything around him, even the most surprising sources.

What else do we learn from the process of writing? What else makes the process itself worthwhile? When we devote ourselves to the hard work of writing, day after day, year after year, lo and behold, we learn how to write. We learn how we write. And we learn what it is that is ours to write.

It was Gay Wilson Allen, in his biography *Waldo Emerson*, who pointed out that even Emerson learned what he needed to write through the process of writing. He did not always know what he wanted to say until he saw it on the page. And often the right words would come to him in the act of writing. Writing is like every other art form in that we learn how to do it by immersing ourselves in the process.

We also learn *courage* — which in my view is absolutely a learned virtue, though Emerson says there is no separate virtue by that name. To Emerson, courage was "the right and healthy state of every man when he is free to do that which is constitutional to him to do. It is directness — the instant performing of that which he ought." I believe what he meant was that it is in the doing that we find our courage — almost as though the doing and the courage are the same thing.

The other learned virtue that emerges in us through the process of writing is perhaps the most valuable of all. We learn to be honest. We grow more honest all the time. Some would say we lose the ability to fool ourselves that we are being honest when we are not. Because what we have written, you see, is right there on the page in front of us. It says — This did not come from you. It came from your tortured efforts to adapt yourself to someone else's idea of who you should be or what you should think or how you should express yourself. Sooner or later we all come to the realization that being who we are, with all of our shortcomings, is the only approach that can bring us any happiness. And not being who we are can only bring regret.

The more we write the more we learn that there is something very freeing about honesty. First of all, we don't have to put near the effort into it that we do into being something we're not. And we don't have to do all the work of wrapping up the package with ribbons and bows. We just offer what we have to give outright and hope it will be valued for what it is.

As we learn to be honest it also becomes harder to fool ourselves about our writing too. We are better able to catch ourselves when we are becoming self-absorbed rather than self-reliant, or when we begin to give way to false martyrdom. We cannot be "candidates for truth" and ever engage in self-pity. We cannot delude ourselves even about why we are unsuccessful as writers. The fact that a lot of great writing goes unappreciated does not mean that all unappreciated writing has merit. It only means it is unappreciated.

In the process of creative writing we do more than discover what we have to give. We discover ourselves. As Emerson said, we unfold ourselves. As we organize and articulate our thoughts we organize and articulate ourselves. We crystallize our values and learn what it is that we truly believe. We even develop new values that were not part of our makeup before we began writing.

When I first committed to writing, for instance, I knew I would have to live very frugally in order to stretch my resources for as long as I could. I was prepared to do this and discovered I was good at it. I lived simply, ate simply, spent money only on necessities, and found my entire social life in conversation with good friends. But I had no idea how I would be changed by my new priorities. I came to understand Emerson's comment about his friend Thoreau that he "chose to be rich by making his wants few." My new life fed me in ways I had not previously been fed. From that time on I could only place the highest value on a simple life.

Yes, there are costs involved in pursuing a creative life. Doris Lessing says we must be honest about this. We must tell aspiring writers how much they have to give up. But it has been my experience that it does not have to be any of the things that truly matter, the most important of which is rich relationships. In fact, I believe writers come to appreciate the people in their lives in a way known only to those who choose such a solitary life.

On this note, I was especially moved by an entry Emerson made in his journal, which Richard Poirier pointed out in his discussion of Emerson's limited "society." Emerson wrote, "...in the rambles of last night's talk with Henry [Thoreau], we stated over and over again, to sadness, almost, the Eternal loneliness ... how insular and pathetically solitary, are all the people we know!" Though I agree with Mr. Poirier that Emerson, like all writers, at times mourned his limited "social resources" — how thoroughly he appreciated the relationships he had! Relationships that were made richer by the deeply shared values that are not always appreciated by a larger society.

In order to pursue a creative life we do have to let go of a lot of the ideas we've been saddled with about what success looks like — about what a successful person does and what they own and how they live their life. Once we've let go of society's notions about success we can begin to discover our own. We can ask our self what it is that will make us feel we are succeeding as a writer.

Every writer who has ever spoken before a group knows that the overriding question in the mind of every aspiring writer in front of them, the one that is invariably the first to be asked is, "How do I get published?" They also know it is pointless to try to unburden anyone of holding up publishing as the ultimate measure of success. Being published is a powerful thing. It can even give us the boost we need in order to keep writing. But I am going to propose an idea that, as radical as it may seem, I hope you will consider.

In addition to giving serious thought to what it is about being published that is so important to us — Is it really the actual publishing, the book we can hold in our hands? Is it the validation it represents? Is it the prospect of reaching others with our thoughts and ideas? — In addition to considering all of the questions we can only benefit from asking ourselves, I urge you to consider this:

You are the one who publishes your writing. You publish it by creating it, by seeing it through to completion, by claiming it as your own. Your work is published when you can hold it in your hands and read it through and know you would not change a single word. The most important publishing that occurs in any writer's life occurs in that moment — the moment we behold a finished work that is the product of our own creative processing.

We often hear of the disparity between the great numbers of people who submit their works to publishers and those who are actually published. What we do not hear about is the much larger gap between the enormous number of people who dream of writing and those who actually do it. Those who get down to the hard work of creating something. This is the real startling minority. And it is the one you most want to be part of. This is where you want to set your sights. Because there is nothing in the world more gratifying than knowing that the drive you felt to write was something real. That you not only experienced it and took it to heart, you acted on it and saw it through.

If I have anything of value to offer you on the subject of publishing it is to urge you to put the idea completely out of your mind. Dismiss it for the entire time it takes you to produce something you know has value — even if it takes many years. I would even say, you will be most fortunate if it does take many years.

What happens when our commitment to writing stretches over years is a deepening of all the relationships that are so important to finding our voice, to *becoming* a writer. We have the great luxury of following our instincts wherever they lead, and of returning to projects after time away from them to approach them with fresh eyes. We are able to explore different genres in order to find the one that really fits, the one in which our voice becomes clear and strong. It is years of writing and experimenting and exploring that teach us the most — about writing, and about what we need to write.

When I first committed to writing, with very little forethought about what I would write, I found myself immersed in a novel. About nine years later, I had completed two. (Or come to the end of two.) The research for those novels, the experience of creating them, I would not trade for any other experience on earth. I learned so much, including about *How Not to Write a Novel*, I have even thought I might one day write a book by this very title. (This will not be one of my future books, though it would be substantive, I assure you.) The most important thing I learned is that through long stretches of writing, through "the sedulous inquiry, day after day, year after year," we do find our way as writers.

If I told you how little effort I have invested in getting those novels published you would probably not believe me. But the truth is, over the past decade and a half, each time I have finished a project, I have come up for air for a day or so, written a single letter to a prospective agent, and plunged right back into my work. I simply could not interrupt the process for any longer than that. Will those works be published? I am confident they will be, when they are ready. But this is even less important to me now than it was when I reached the end of those books. What remains the most important thing is remaining *in the process.*

As I said early on, I was compelled to write this book because of the joy I have experienced in my own creative work. "Joy" is not a word any of us has a lot of opportunity to use. And yet this is the feeling I have experienced consistently in the process of creative writing, in the opportunity to "breathe and to live on illustrious thoughts."

But how can we commit to years of writing in the mere hope of producing something with its own intrinsic value? How can we adopt such priorities and even justify our existence? — to ourselves, to the people we love? Here again we come to the heart of "Emersonian creative writing." Emerson persuades us that to be a "candidate for truth" is socially justified even when there are no practical results at all. He assures us that contemplative achievements are equal in dignity to the noblest recognized profession. He even guides us to our own deep understanding of the discoveries he made as a creative writer — that we "find the journey's end in every step of the road" — and "Expression *is* prosperity!"

What any creative endeavor teaches us is that it is not only important to continually reexamine our ideas about success, but also to recognize that success sometimes comes to us in forms other than those we imagined. The skies do not part, but we do experience some amazing sunsets.

The experience of a single moment of inspiration, all by itself, can make sense out of years of yearning, years of struggle. And the opportunity to watch a written work take form, as Vivian Hopkins described it, "with the same mixture of mystery and calculation which prevails in the combination of chemical atoms" — this is a sunset beyond description. All throughout the process we experience moments of such astonishment and wonder we become convinced we are not so much creating as uncovering thoughts, thoughts that have been placed there just for us. We come to understand what Emerson meant when he said, "we are here not to work but to be worked upon."

We also experience a new sense of progress. Real progress, the kind that makes our blood move. That drives us continually toward a completion at the same time we do not want the process to ever end. There is no sense of progress more real, more enriching or invigorating than the one we come to know in the process of creating.

And what is the greatest sense of progress we experience as creative writers, especially over years? The more we give to the process, the more we are drawn into it and the more it leads us on our own journey of discovery. After a while we find we have become so absorbed, so distracted by our pure fascination with the process, we are unwittingly led into our own expression. The expression Emerson says is nothing less than the completion of our selves.

Whenever we commit to anything that requires long hard effort, it is the inner rewards that are our highest gains. Because they are the ones that become part of us. They enrich us in ways that no external reward can. In the process of creative writing, the greatest inner reward is that we learn self-reliance. We learn it in a way that only the creative process can teach us. This alone can make years of hard effort a small price to pay.

And there is something else that happens when we spend years absorbed in creative processing. Our sights begin to reach beyond our own personal yearnings. What began as a striving for meaning and purpose in our life becomes a longing for meaning and purpose in all of life. We even begin to understand how Emerson came to believe that if we all had rich inner lives we would all come to appreciate the sacredness of life. We would all work together to protect and to care for one another and to preserve our world for future generations. When we are fortunate enough to live a creative life we cannot help believing in the possibility of such a world.

It may well be that we will never achieve anything more than our own vision of a world that works. But if Emerson and the other great minds have been getting the messages right, the vision alone, in one individual, is a powerful thing.

Among the many things Emerson has given me is a deep feeling of certainty about the value of what I do every day, even when it seems there is little understanding of its value outside of the people closest to me. He has persuaded me that I am a successful writer as long as I continue to follow where my soul leads and to learn everything writing has to teach me. And if in the process I can inspire a single other person to do the same, then I will have been a worthy instrument. I will have contributed something valuable to the world.

As Emerson said, "We are always getting ready to live, but never living." And who has not felt this to be true? By devoting ourselves to creative writing we are able to know in the deepest part of ourselves that we are "exercising the highest functions of human nature." We are able to look back and to know with certainty that the time we have spent writing has been time we have truly lived.

You will hear every day … that the first duty is to get land and money, place and name. 'What is this Truth you seek? What is this Beauty?' men will ask, with derision. If, nevertheless, God has called you to explore truth and beauty, be bold, be firm, be true.

When you shall say … I must eat the good of the land and let learning and romantic expectations go … then dies the man in you; then once more perish the buds of art and poetry … as they have died already in a thousand thousand men.

The hour of that choice is the crisis of your history … Bend to the persuasion which is flowing to you from every object of nature, to be its tongue to the heart of man.

Ralph Waldo Emerson

Notes & Acknowledgements

In identifying for the reader the quotes contained in this book, it was important to me to acknowledge my actual sources. Without the work of the many scholars who have devoted lifetimes to understanding Emerson, I would not have uncovered much of the wealth of Emersonian wisdom which is found beyond Emerson's most familiar works, his Essays — in his journals, lectures, letters, and other writings. In each of the biographies, critical studies and selected collections I read, I found both new Emersonian jewels and new jewels of insight to Emerson's thought. For this, I am tremendously indebted and deeply grateful to the scholars and writers acknowledged here.

Emerson quotes are clearly noted: **RWE**

"**A man should learn to detect and watch that gleam of light which flashes across his mind from within.**" **RWE** "Self Reliance," *Essays, First Series*

What is Creative Writing?

"**It seemed to me as if I had written the book myself in some former life...**" **RWE** Edward Waldo Emerson, *Emerson in Concord: A Memoir*, 1888, Houghton Mifflin Company, p. 29

"**Cut these words and they would bleed...**"**It happens to us once or twice in a lifetime, to be drunk with some book...**" **RWE** Robert D. Richardson, *First We Read Then We Write: Emerson on the Creative Process*, 2009, University of Iowa Press, p. 33, 9

Creative Reading

"**First we eat, then we beget, first we read then we write.**" **RWE** *Emerson in His Journals*, Selected and Edited by Joel Porte, 1982, The Belknap Press of Harvard University, p.298 (Dec. 1842-Jan.1843)

"**epicure at a long table ...**" Stephen E. Whicher, *Freedom and Fate: An Inner Life of Ralph Waldo Emerson*, 1953, University of Pennsylvania Press, p.28

"**what American miners call a 'high-grader'...pockets only the richest lumps of ore.**" Robert D. Richardson, *First We Read Then We Write: Emerson on the Creative Process*, 2009, University of Iowa Press, p. 8

Who is Emerson?

"**America's philosopher**" Philip F. Gura, *American Transcendentalism*, 2007, Hill and Wang, Farrar, Straus & Giroux

"**the first philosopher of the American spirit**" Brooks Atkinson, Biographical Introduction, *The Selected Writings of Ralph Waldo Emerson*, 1940, The Modern Library, Random House, Inc.

"**the purest of American seers**" Paul Elmer More, *The Cambridge History of English and American Literature*, 18 vols., 1907-1921, vol. XV

"**the dominant sage of the American imagination**" Harold Bloom, "The Sage of Concord," *The Guardian*, May 23, 2003

"**He belonged by nature to that mystical company of devout souls...**" George Santayana, "Emerson," 1900, *Interpretations of Poetry and Religion*

"**golden age of oratory**" Lawrence Buell, *Emerson*, 2003, Belknap Press of Harvard University, p.116

"**the movement borrowed its inspiration more from him...**" Oliver Wendell Holmes, *Ralph Waldo Emerson*, 1885, Houghton Mifflin and Company, p.147

"**The Transcendentalists recognized their own individuality because they shared a consciousness which valued it**" Catherine Albanese, *Corresponding Motion: Transcendental Religion and the New America*, 1977, Temple University Press, p.xxiii

"**He answered Tolstoi's demand for essential greatness — he had no kinks.**" Lewis Mumford, *The Golden Day: A Study in American Literature and Culture*, 1926, W. W. Norton & Co., p.102

"**We walk about in a sleep. A few moments...in our lifetime, we truly live.**" RWE Stephen E. Whicher, *Freedom and Fate: An Inner Life of Ralph Waldo Emerson*, 1953, University of Pennsylvania Press, p.30 (Journal, Jan, 1842)

"**I should like to...do nothing for which I had not the whole world for my reason.**" RWE James Elliot Cabot, *A Memoir of Ralph Waldo Emerson*, 1887, Houghton Mifflin Co., p.437

"**If anything, Emerson believed too much, not too little.**" Robert D. Richardson, Jr., *Emerson: The Mind on Fire*, 1995, University of California Press, p.125

"**Religion... It is the order and soundness of a man.**" RWE *The Heart of Emerson's Journals*, Edited by Bliss Perry, 1909, Houghton Mifflin Co., p 57 (July, 1832)

"**the conservatism of politics reinforced the conservatism of religion...**" John Jay Chapman, "Emerson," *Emerson and Other Essays*, 1898, NY Scribner's Sons

"**You don't get a candle to see the sunrise.**" RWE *Selections from Ralph Waldo Emerson: An Organic Anthology*, Edited by Stephen E. Whicher, 1957, Houghton Mifflin Co., p. 10 (Oct, 1832)

"**Emerson brought into the service of the religious instinct...**" O.W. Firkins, *Ralph Waldo Emerson*, 1915, Houghton Mifflin Company, p.307

"**no man should be admitted whose presence excluded...the only guest not tolerated...**" Philip F. Gura, *American Transcendentalism: A History*, 2007, Hill and Wang, Farrar, Strauss and Giroux, p. 70, 5

"**to assert the disappointing incompleteness of ideology itself.**" Randall Fuller, *Emerson's Ghosts: Literature, Politics and the Making of Americanists*, 2007, Oxford University Press, p.17

"What is a man born for but to be a Reformer, a Remaker of what man has made?" RWE Richard Geldard, *The Spiritual Teachings of Ralph Waldo Emerson*, 2001, Lindisfarne Books, p.1 ("Man the Reformer" 1841)

Jeanne de Vietinghoff, ***The Understanding of Good*** 2016 reissue of the book available through Gleam of Light Press

Olive Schreiner quote: Lawrence Buell, *Emerson*, 2003, Belknap Press of Harvard, p.47

Margaret Fuller quote: Octavius Brooks Frothingham, *Transcendentalism in New England: A History* (1876) 1965, Peter Smith, Gloucester, MA, p.312

Maurice Maeterlinck quote: "Emerson" (1898) *Ralph Waldo Emerson, Bloom's Classic Critical Views*, 2008, Infobase Publishing, p.87 (Note: text differs from 1912 version, *Emerson and Other Essays* by Maurice Maeterlinck)

"Emerson provided a new impetus and direction for thought and writing..." Joel Porte, *Representative Man: Ralph Waldo Emerson in His Time*, 1979, Oxford University Press, p.vii

"Every major critical trend in American literary study since 1900..." Joel Myerson, *A Historical Guide to Ralph Waldo Emerson*, 2000, New York Oxford University Press, p.3

"From his moment to ours, American authors either are in his tradition..." Harold Bloom, *Ralph Waldo Emerson, Bloom's Modern Critical Views*, 2007, Chelsea House Publishers, p.1

"Emerson is with me daily, more frequently even as I age..." Harold Bloom, *Ralph Waldo Emerson, Bloom's Classic Critical Views*, 2008, Infobase Publishing, p.xii

"If it persuades others that Emerson is worth pondering for so long a time..." Lawrence Buell, *Emerson*, 2003, Belknap Press of Harvard University, p. 6

"that which is for him to say lies as a load on his heart until it is delivered." RWE *Representative Men*, "Goethe; or, The Writer"

"He wishes to give us to ourselves." Harold Bloom, *Ralph Waldo Emerson, Bloom's Modern Critical Views*, 2007, Chelsea House Publishers, p.2 (Note: RWE: "That is always best which gives me to myself." "Divinity School Address" 1838)

"Emerson, who knew that the only literary and critical method was oneself..." Harold Bloom, *Ralph Waldo Emerson, Bloom's Modern Critical Views*, 2007, Chelsea House Publishers, p.12

"If our dormant intuition answers to his, we are profoundly kindled and confirmed..." Paul Elmer More, *The Cambridge History of English and American Literature*, 1907-1921, vol. XV

"For those who need an atmosphere for wings..." Octavius Brooks Frothingham, *Transcendentalism in New England: A History* (1876) 1965, Peter Smith, Gloucester, MA, p.248, 221

"every strong American thinker and writer has been an Emersonian or an anti-Emersonian..." Harold Bloom, *Ralph Waldo Emerson, Bloom's Classic Critical Views*, 2008, Infobase Publishing, p. xi

Notes to Pages 22 to 25

"life is strange enough, profound enough, great enough..." Maurice Maeterlinck, "Emerson" (1898) *Ralph Waldo Emerson, Bloom's Classic Critical Views*, 2008, Infobase Publishing, p.87 (Note: text differs from the 1912 version, *Emerson and Other Essays* by Maurice Maeterlinck)

"**Emersonian thought was not a minor, Romantic trend...**" Richard G. Geldard, *God in Concord: Ralph Waldo Emerson's Awakening to the Infinite*, 1999, Larson Publications, p.157

"**The lengthened shadow of our American culture is Emerson's...**" Harold Bloom, "Emerson: The American Religion," *Ralph Waldo Emerson, Bloom's Modern Critical Views*, 2007, Chelsea House Publishers, p.33

"**a great American...who understood as well as any...**" Perry Miller, "Emersonian Genius and the American Democracy," *The New England Quarterly*, Mar. 1953 (later version in his book *Errand into the Wilderness*, 1956, Belknap Press of Harvard University)

"**The promise of America...had seeped into every pore of Emerson's mind.**" Lewis Mumford, *The Golden Day: A Study in American Literature and Culture*, 1926, W. W. Norton & Co., p.105

"**fill the postponed expectation of the world...Who can doubt, that poetry will revive and lead in a new age...**" RWE "The American Scholar" 1837

"**It seems so easy for America to inspire and express... It is the country of the Future.**" RWE Gay Wilson Allen, *Waldo Emerson: A Biography*, 1981, Viking Press New York, p. 422 ("The Young American" 1844)

"**It is finally not a matter of word-making alone but of life-making and world-making as well.**" Lawrence Buell, *Emerson*, 2003, Belknap Press of Harvard University, p. 108

Horace Mann scene Ralph L. Rusk, *The Life of Ralph Waldo Emerson*, 1949, Charles Scribner's Sons, p. 247

"**Emerson believed in the dignity of human life...**" Stephen E. Whicher, *Freedom and Fate: An Inner Life of Ralph Waldo Emerson*, 1953, University of Pennsylvania Press, p.173

"**In him, philosophy resumed the full gamut of human experience...**" Lewis Mumford, *The Golden Day: A Study in American Literature and Culture*, 1926, W. W. Norton & Co., p.102

"**the world's eye...the world's heart**" RWE "The American Scholar" 1837

Art is the need to create... Nothing less than the creation of man and nature is its end." RWE "Art," *Essays, First Series*

"**Emerson was a sort of living essence**" Lewis Mumford, *The Golden Day: A Study in American Literature and Culture*, 1926, W. W. Norton & Co., NY, p.95

"**His sincerity marked him as a visitant from a higher sphere.**" Lawrence Buell, *Emerson*, 2003, Belknap Press of Harvard University, p. 312

"**he habitually dwelt in that ampler and diviner air...**" Oliver Wendell Holmes, *Ralph Waldo Emerson*, 1885, Houghton Mifflin Co., p. 361

"**If we must define him in one word, we have to call him Artist.**" William James' Address at the Emerson Centenary Celebration, Concord, MA, 1903

Reading Emerson

"**Not every man can read them, but they will reward him who can.**" RWE *Representative Men*: "Swedenborg; or, The Mystic"

"**Emerson stood for...a freer thought and expression than American literature... had yet known.**" Edward Waldo Emerson, *Emerson in Concord: A Memoir*, 1888, Houghton Mifflin Company, p. 89

"**I can no more manage these thoughts that come into my head than thunderbolts.**" RWE *Emerson in His Journals*, Selected and Edited by Joel Porte, 1982, The Belknap Press of Harvard University, p. 478 (July-Aug.1857)

"**he succeeded in delivering himself of his thought...**" John Jay Chapman, "Emerson," *Emerson and Other Essays*, 1898, NY Scribner's Sons

"**Thinking, for Emerson, was not...a special activity...Because he was distracted by little else...**" Stephen E. Whicher, *Selections from Ralph Waldo Emerson: An Organic Anthology*, 1957, Houghton Mifflin Co., p. 1, xiii

"**the action of a superior imagination...taking possession of its world.**" Stephen E. Whicher, *Freedom and Fate: An Inner Life of Ralph Waldo Emerson*, 1953, University of Pennsylvania Press, p.173

"**an extraordinary effect of exaltation...**" Virginia Woolf, "Emerson's Journals," *Books and Portraits*, 1977, Harcourt Brace Jovanovich

"**primitive poetry of the soul**" Philip F. Gura, *American Transcendentalism*, 2007, Hill and Wang, Farrar, Straus & Giroux, p.44

"**inimitable, unattainable by talent, as if caught from some dream**" RWE Evelyn Barish, *Emerson: Roots of Prophecy*, 1989, Princeton University Press, p. 135

"**Sublimity of motive must precede sublimity of style.**" Evelyn Barish, *Emerson: Roots of Prophecy*, 1989, Princeton University Press, p. 109

"**It was one of the richest and most beautiful compositions...**" Walter Whitman, *New York Aurora*, March 7, 1842, *Ralph Waldo Emerson, Bloom's Classic Critical Views*, Edited and Introduced by Harold Bloom, 2008, Infobase Publishing, p.157

"**James A. Garfield, later a President of the United States...**" Ralph L. Rusk, *The Life of Ralph Waldo Emerson*, 1949, Charles Scribner's Sons, p. 385

James Russell Lowell: "**There was a tone in it that awakened all elevating associations...**" H.B. Van Wesep, *Seven Sages: The Story of American Philosophy*, 1960, David McKay Company, Inc., p. 64

"'**inwardly and desperately drunk' with conviction**" RWE F.O. Matthiessen, *American Renaissance: Art and Expression in the Age of Emerson and Whitman*, 1941, Oxford University Press, p.17

"**He enters immediately into universal truth.**" F.O. Matthiessen, *American Renaissance: Art and Expression in the age of Emerson and Whitman*, 1941, Oxford University Press, p.18

"The utter want and loss of all method..." RWE *Selections from Ralph Waldo Emerson: An Organic Anthology*, Edited by Stephen E. Whicher, 1957, Houghton Mifflin Co., p. 59 (March 1837)

"of sentences that lie upon the page like steel filings..." Barbara L. Packer, *Emerson's Fall: A New Interpretation of the Major Essays*, 1982, Continuum International Publishing, p. 7

Parker: "an army all officers..." Charles J. Woodbury, *Talks with Emerson*, first pub. 1890, Horizon Press NY, 1970, p. 149

Lowell: "a chaos filled with shooting stars" John McAleer, *Ralph Waldo Emerson: Days of Encounter*, 1984, Little Brown & Co., p. 5

"Where they fail to reach the reader's heart..." Paul Elmer More, *The Cambridge History of English and American Literature*, 1907-1921, vol. XV

"only boards and logs tied together" RWE F.O. Matthiessen, *American Renaissance: Art and Expression in the age of Emerson and Whitman*, 1941, Oxford University Press, p. 64 (Emerson to Carlyle just before the appearance of his first essays, 1841)

"If Minerva offered me a gift and an option..." RWE *Emerson in His Journals*, Selected and Edited by Joel Porte, 1982, The Belknap Press of Harvard University, p. 454 (May, 1854)

"so passionate and alive, that like the spirit of a plant or an animal..." RWE "The Poet," *Essays, Second Series*

"Emerson called his own sentences, 'infinitely repellent particles...'" Van Wyck Brooks, *America's Coming of Age* (1915) 1958, Doubleday Anchor Books, p.38

"Churchman and Agnostic could each find in his writings an armory of weapons..." Edward Waldo Emerson, *Emerson in Concord: A Memoir*, 1888, Houghton Mifflin Company, p. 248

"He insists that even though he may feel in the grip of the Truth..." Lawrence Buell, *Emerson*, 2003, Belknap Press of Harvard University, p. 312

"He in whom the love of truth predominates..." RWE "Intellect," *Essays, First Series*

"The truest state of mind, rested in, becomes false." RWE *Emerson in His Journals*, Selected and Edited by Joel Porte, 1982, The Belknap Press of Harvard University, p.138 (May 1835)

"every moment of the existence of the universe as a new creation." James Elliot Cabot, *A Memoir of Ralph Waldo Emerson*, 1887, Houghton Mifflin Co., p. 159

"his mind...is conspicuously valuable" for its flexibility and variety and even its contradictions..." Ralph L. Rusk, *The Life of Ralph Waldo Emerson*, 1949, Charles Scribner's Sons, p. viii

"I know no more irreconcilable persons ever brought to annoy & confound each other..." RWE *Emerson in His Journals, Selected and Edited by Joel Porte*, 1982, The Belknap Press of Harvard University, p. 491 (Jan-Feb., 1861)

"Speak what you think to-day in words as hard as cannon balls..." RWE "Self Reliance," *Essays, First Series*

"What is a man born for but to be a Reformer..." **RWE** David M. Robinson, *The Political Emerson*, 2004, Beacon Press ("Man the Reformer," 1841)

"So I will forget my yesterdays and hear only the sweet bells of today." **RWE** *The Selected Letters of Ralph Waldo Emerson*, Edited by Joel Myerson, 1997, Columbia University Press, p. 207 (to Margaret Fuller, 1840)

"A foolish consistency is the hobgoblin of little minds." **RWE** "Self Reliance," *Essays, First Series*

"The struggle of his life taught him not to deny uncertainty..." Evelyn Barish, *Emerson: The Roots of Prophecy*, 1989, Princeton University Press, p. 8

"doubt seems to him the height and the end of wisdom; to Emerson it is only the means." James Elliot Cabot, A *Memoir of Ralph Waldo Emerson*, 1887, Houghton Mifflin Co., p.326

"the compulsions and conflicts, the revelations and doubts..." Stephen E. Whicher, *Freedom and Fate: An Inner Life of Ralph Waldo Emerson*, 1953, University of Pennsylvania Press, p.173

"champion of the royal virtue of honest inconsistency" Jay William Hudson, "The Religion of Emerson," *The Sewanee Review*, vol. 28, Apr. 1, 1920

"He was only noting single aspects of truth as they struck him..." James Elliot Cabot, *A Memoir of Ralph Waldo Emerson*, 1887, Houghton Mifflin Company, p.626

"He had the poet's gift of turning far, abstract thoughts into..." Virginia Woolf, "Emerson's Journals," *Books and Portraits*, 1977, Harcourt Brace Jovanovich

"Emerson consistently and utterly expressed himself..." John Jay Chapman, "Emerson," *Emerson and Other Essays*, 1898, NY Scribner's Sons

"If a man would be anything, he must be himself." Lawrence Buell, *Emerson*, 2003, Belknap Press of Harvard University, p. 46 (Walt Whitman described Emerson's "The American Scholar" as "a statement of primary things," especially, that "if a man would be anything, he must be himself.")

"As a steady force in the transmutation of life into ideas..." Paul Elmer More, *The Cambridge History of English and American Literature*, 1907–1921, vol. XV

"The briefest way, finally, to cut through to an understanding...is to remember where he always threw his last emphasis." F.O. Matthiessen, *American Renaissance: Art and Expression in the age of Emerson and Whitman*, 1941, Oxford University Press, p. 54

Horace Mann: "It was almost impossible to catch the great beauty and proportion of one truth..." Ralph L. Rusk, *The Life of Ralph Waldo Emerson*, 1949, Charles Scribner's Sons, p.247

"its highest effect is to make new artists." **RWE**, "Art," *Essays, First Series*

Self Reliance

"I will not live out of me/ I will not see with others' eyes..." **RWE** Robert D. Richardson, Jr., *Emerson: Mind on Fire*, 1995, University of California Press, p. 126 (the beginning of a poem RWE wrote in his Journal, Oct 1832) "**immeasurably high standard...which nothing else in education could supply**" **RWE** Edward Waldo Emerson, *Emerson in Concord: A Memoir*, 1888, Houghton Mifflin Co, p. 10

"**Emerson did not shine in the things Harvard then knew how to measure.**" Robert D. Richardson, Jr., *Emerson: Mind on Fire*, 1995, University of California Press, p. 6

"**Education is the drawing out of the Soul.**" **RWE** *Emerson in His Journals*, Selected and Edited by Joel Porte, 1982, The Belknap Press of Harvard University, p. 80 (Sept.13, 1831)

"**Emerson used his favorite self-identifying term, scholar, in a disruptively anti-professional sense...**" Lawrence Buell, *Emerson*, 2003, Belknap Press of Harvard University, p. 8

"**Emerson is confident that within each man or woman lies a 'genius'...True scholarship sets this genius free.**" Russell B. Goodman, *American Philosophy and the Romantic Tradition*, 1990, Cambridge University Press, p. 36

"**all our education aims to sink what is individual or personal in us**" **RWE** Robert D. Richardson, Jr., *Emerson: Mind on Fire,* 1995, University of California Press, p. 258 (Concord Address, August 1844)

"**to teach self-trust**" **RWE** Lawrence Buell, *Emerson*, 2003, Belknap Press of Harvard University, p. 294

"**The aim of education is to 'keep' the child's 'nature and arm it with knowledge in the very direction...**" **RWE** *Stanford Encyclopedia of Philosophy*: Ralph Waldo Emerson

"**Here was a young man who demanded that the preacher...**" Gay Wilson Allen, *Waldo Emerson: A Biography*, 1981, Viking Press New York, p.106

"**we do not make a world of our own, but fall into institutions already made...**" **RWE** Ralph L. Rusk, *The Life of Ralph Waldo Emerson*, 1949, Charles Scribner's Sons, p.159

"**the whole of our social structure — State, School, Religion...**" **RWE** James Elliot Cabot, *A Memoir of RWE*, 1887, Houghton Mifflin Co., p.436

"**The faith that stands on authority is not faith.**" **RWE** "The Over-Soul," *Essays, First Series*

"**Faith makes us, and not we it, and faith makes its own forms**" **RWE** "Divinity School Address" 1838

"**for all our soul-destroying slavery to habit...**" **RWE** "Divinity School Address" 1838

"**Religion was her occupation...**" **RWE** Evelyn Barish, *Emerson: The Roots of Prophecy*, 1989, Princeton University Press, p. 53 (JMN 5:323-4)

"**I have sometimes thought that to be a good minister it was necessary to leave the ministry.**" **RWE** Edward Waldo Emerson, *Emerson in Concord: A Memoir*, 1888, Houghton Mifflin Company, p. 42

"**Emerson had left the pulpit for the lecturers desk...**" James Elliot Cabot, *A Memoir of Ralph Waldo Emerson*, 1887, Houghton Mifflin Company, p.397

"It is as if a man had been withdrawn from the earth..." John Jay Chapman, "Emerson," *Emerson and Other Essays*, 1898, NY Scribner's Sons

"self-reliance means, precisely, the readiness to treat with sympathetic understanding ..." George Kateb, *Emerson and Self-Reliance*, 1995, Sage Publications, p.4

"The one thing in the world of value is the active soul..." RWE "The American Scholar" 1837

"Emerson's ultimate meaning of self-reliance is to be properly religious." George Kateb, *Emerson and Self-Reliance*, 1995, Sage Publications, p.17 (Note: RWE: "self-reliance, the height and perfection of man, is reliance on God" ("The Fugitive Slave Law," 1854)

"For Emerson, genuine individualism was not narcissism or monomania..." Wesley T. Mott, "The Age of the First Person Singular": Emerson and Individualism, *A Historical Guide to Ralph Waldo Emerson*, Edited by Joel Myerson, 2000, Oxford University Press, p. 91

"The soul stipulates for no private good..." RWE David M. Robinson, "Emerson and Religion," *A Historical Guide to Ralph Waldo Emerson*, Edited by Joel Myerson, 2000, Oxford University Press, p. 173

"The soul knows no persons." RWE George Edward Woodberry, *Ralph Waldo Emerson*, 1907, The Macmillan Company, p.56

"The more inward you go, the less individuated you get." Lawrence Buell, *Emerson*, 2003, Belknap Press of Harvard University, p.65

"In listening more intently to our own reason..." RWE *Emerson in His Journals*, Selected and Edited by Joel Porte, 1982, The Belknap Press of Harvard University, p. 71 (Sept. 27-28, 1830)

"A trust in yourself is the height not of pride, but of piety..." RWE Ralph L. Rusk, *The Life of Ralph Waldo Emerson*, 1949, Charles Scribner's Sons, p.158 (133rd sermon)

"'Live from within'— was not a means of carefree liberation..." Stephen E. Whicher, *Freedom and Fate: An Inner Life of Ralph Waldo Emerson*, 1953, University of Pennsylvania Press, p.59

"If any one imagines that this law is lax, let him keep its commandment one day." RWE "Self- Reliance," *Essays, First Series*

"It would overturn society and resolve the world into chaos...Harriet Martineau wrote to America..." Ralph L. Rusk, *The Life of Ralph Waldo Emerson*, 1949, Charles Scribner's Sons, p. 284-5

"Men are what their mother's make them." RWE John McAleer, *Ralph Waldo Emerson: Days of Encounter*, 1984, Little Brown & Co., p.21

Carlyle: "Ah! the dear Emerson!..." Thomas Wentworth Higginson, *A Part of a Man's Life*, 1905, Houghton, Mifflin and Co., p.2

"self-reliance has more to do with self-surrender than self-enlargement... shaped by underlying humility." David Robinson, *The Spiritual Emerson: Essential Writings*, 2003, Beacon Press, p.84, 21

"There is no integrity in rebellion per se." Richard Geldard, *The Spiritual Teachings of Ralph Waldo Emerson*, 2001, Lindisfarne Books, p. 176

The Gleam of Light

"the soul within which every man's particular being is contained and made one with all other..." RWE "The Over-Soul" *Essays, First Series*

"for which all things exist, and that by which they are" RWE *Nature*

"Emerson asserts that the artist...attains direct contact..." Vivian C. Hopkins, S*pires of Form: A Study of Emerson's Aesthetic Theory*, 1951, Harvard University Press, p.9

"Over Soul," a translation of the Sanskrit 'At-Man'..." Gay Wilson Allen, *Waldo Emerson: A Biography*, 1981, Viking Press New York, p. xi

"We belong to it, not it to us." RWE David M. Robinson, *The Spiritual Emerson: Essential Writings*, 2003, Beacon Press, p.244 ("Character" 1866)

"one universal Artist back of all artists" Ralph L. Rusk, *The Life of Ralph Waldo Emerson*, 1949, Charles Scribner's Sons, p.283

"All things are known to the soul." RWE "The Method of Nature" 1841

"There is in all great poets a wisdom of humanity which is superior to any talents they exercise." RWE "The Over-Soul," *Essays, First Series*

"We all depend at last on the few heads...nearest the stars." RWE *Emerson in His Journals*, Selected and Edited by Joel Porte, 1982, The Belknap Press of Harvard, p. 453 (Feb 1854)

"Get books that will open your eyes & your ears..." RWE *Emerson in His Journals*, Selected and Edited by Joel Porte, 1982, The Belknap Press, p. 569 (July 1873)

"Take thankfully and heartily all they can give...Exhaust them, wrestle with them..." RWE "Intellect," *Essays, First Series*

"Great works of art...no kernel of nourishing corn can come to him but through his toil bestowed on that plot of ground which is given to him to till." RWE "Self Reliance," *Essays, First Series*

"The woods were his best study... even in winter storms..." Edward Waldo Emerson, *Emerson in Concord: A Memoir*, 1888, Houghton Mifflin Company, p. 63, 256

"We lie in the lap of immense intelligence..." RWE "Self Reliance," *Essays, First Series*

"Place yourself in the middle of the stream of power and wisdom..." RWE "Spiritual Laws," *Essays, First Series*

"sympathetic identification...a being alive within an organic scene...merged with the totality..." Jonathan Bishop, *Emerson on the Soul*, 1964, Harvard University Press, p. 28-9

"The world is...of one will, of one mind ... All things proceed out of the same spirit, and all things conspire with it." RWE "Divinity School Address" 1838

"My friends...the Great God gave them to me...High thanks I owe to you..." RWE Richard G. Geldard, *God in Concord: Ralph Waldo Emerson's Awakening to the Infinite*, 1999, Larson Publications, p.140 ("Friends")

"a series of intoxications...the true school of philosophy...angles of vision." RWE Charles J. Woodbury, *Talks with Emerson* (1890) 1970, Horizon Press NY, p.96

"No man believes any more than he has experienced." RWE *Emerson in His Journals*, Selected and Edited by Joel Porte, 1982, The Belknap Press, p.304 (Mar.-Apr., 1843)

"The scholar loses no hour which the man lives..." RWE "The American Scholar" 1837

"All our experience is thus convertible into jewels." RWE *Emerson in His Journals*, Selected and Edited by Joel Porte, 1982, The Belknap Press of Harvard University, p. 152 (Oct 1836)

"Life is our dictionary...Drudgery, calamity, exasperation..." RWE "The American Scholar" 1837

"The gardener saves every slip, and seed..." RWE *Representative Men*, "Goethe; or, The Writer"

"His needs, appetites, talents, affections, accomplishments..." RWE "Literary Ethics" 1838

"Their success lay in their parallelism to the course of thought which found in them an unobstructed channel." RWE "Spiritual Laws," *Essays, First Series*

"The joy which will not let me sit in my chair..." RWE *Emerson in His Journals*, Selected and Edited by Joel Porte, 1982, The Belknap Press of Harvard University, p. 486 (Aug. 16-19, 1859)

"There is no miracle so stupendous as this moment's health..." RWE Vivian C. Hopkins, *Spires of Form: A Study of Emerson's Aesthetic Theory*, 1951, Harvard University Press, p.19 (ms. journals, 1869)

"...When the devout motions of the soul come, yield to them heart and life." RWE "Self Reliance," *Essays, First Series*

Becoming a Writer

"There is no way to learn to write except by writing." RWE Charles J. Woodbury, *Talks with Emerson* (1890), 1970, Horizon Press NY, p. 139

"Those who have written best are not those who have known most..." RWE *Emerson in His Journals*, Selected and Edited by Joel Porte, 1982, The Belknap Press of Harvard University, p. 256 (July-Aug. 1841)

Finding Your Voice

"The way to speak and write what shall not go out of fashion..." RWE "Spiritual Laws," *Essays, First Series*

"the joy of uttering what no other can utter" RWE F.O. Matthiessen, *American Renaissance: Art and Expression in the age of Emerson and Whitman*, 1941, Oxford University Press, p.17

"He has not learned the lesson of life who does not every day surmount a fear." RWE Richard Geldard, *The Spiritual Teachings of Ralph Waldo Emerson*, 2001, Lindisfarne Books, p.146 ("Courage")

"Always do what you are afraid to do." Edward Waldo Emerson, *Emerson in Concord: A Memoir*, 1888, Houghton Mifflin Company, p.10

"Literature is the record of all; the sum and measure of humanity..." **RWE** Vivian C. Hopkins, *Spires of Form: A Study of Emerson's Aesthetic Theory*, 1951, Harvard University Press, p.105 ("Literature" 1836)

"A man's style is his intellectual Voice only in part under his control. It has its own proper tone and manner which when he is not thinking of it, it will always assume." **RWE** Evelyn Barish, *Emerson: The Roots of Prophecy*, 1989, Princeton University Press, p.215-16 (JMN 3:26)

"the more truly he consults his own powers, the more difference will his work exhibit from the work of any other." **RWE** "Spiritual Laws," *Essays, First Series*

"We know the truth...as we know when we are awake that we are awake. **RWE** "The Over Soul," *Essays, First Series*

Shutting Out the Other Voices

"It is easy to live for others; everybody does. I call on you to live for yourself." **RWE** *The Later Lectures of Ralph Waldo Emerson*, 1843-1871, vol. 1, Edited by Ronald A. Bosco and Joel Myerson, 2010, University of Georgia Press, p.97 ("Two Discourses" 1845)

"the secret of his stimulating power...He knows that we are full of genius..." John Jay Chapman, "Emerson," *Emerson and Other Essays*, 1898, NY Scribner's Sons

"What I must do is all that concerns me, not what the people think...Do your work and you shall reinforce yourself." **RWE** "Self-Reliance" *Essays, First Series*

"Happy is he who looks only into his work to know if it will succeed..."**RWE** *The Heart of Emerson's Journals*, Edited by Bliss Perry, 1909, Houghton Mifflin Co., p.231 (April 1848)

"dream-like anticipations of greatness." **RWE** Evelyn Barish, *Emerson: The Roots of Prophecy*, 1989, Princeton University Press, p. 72 (letter to Aunt Mary at age eighteen)

"Emerson never seems to have given a moment's thought to the prospect of permanent fame..." Lawrence Buell, *Emerson*, 2003, Belknap Press of Harvard University, p. 319

"Matthew Arnold said, "Emerson was a friend and aider of those who would live in the spirit." Richard Geldard, *The Spiritual Teachings of Ralph Waldo Emerson*, 2001, Lindisfarne Books, p. 21

"out of equilibrium...in a false position to people...It spoils thought." **RWE** *Emerson in His Journals*, Selected and Edited by Joel Porte, 1982, The Belknap Press of Harvard University, p.196 (Sept 1838)

"Society's praise can be cheaply secured" **RWE** "Divinity School Address" 1838

"If a man has good corn..." **RWE** *Selections from Ralph Waldo Emerson: An Organic Anthology*, Edited by Stephen E. Whicher, 1957, Houghton Mifflin Co., p. 361 (Feb 1855)

"Amputate!... Say it! Out with it! Search unweariedly..." **RWE** Charles J. Woodbury, *Talks with Emerson*, first pub. 1890, Horizon Press NY, 1970, p. 23

"Truth was more felt than thought out..." Gay Wilson Allen, *Waldo Emerson: A Biography*, 1981, Viking Press New York, p.162

"To Emerson, perception was more potent than reasoning." John Dewey, "Emerson: The Philosopher of Democracy," read at the Emerson Memorial Meeting, University of Chicago, May 25, 1903, *International Journal of Ethics*, vol. 13, no. 4

"It was clear to him that the origin of his knowledge lay in human feeling." Evelyn Barish, *Emerson: Roots of Prophecy*, 1989, Princeton University Press, p. 115

"What is a man good for without enthusiasm..." RWE *Emerson in His Journals*, Selected and Edited by Joel Porte, 1982, The Belknap Press of Harvard University, p.178 (Aug 1847)

"All excellence is only an inflamed personality." RWE *The Selected Lectures of Ralph Waldo Emerson*, Edited by Ronald A. Bosco and Joel Myerson, 2005, University of Georgia Press, p. 146 ("The Tendencies and Duties of Men of Thought," 1848-1850)

Be the fanatic of your subject..." RWE *Emerson in His Journals*, Selected and Edited by Joel Porte, 1982, The Belknap Press of Harvard University, p.485 (May 1859)

"Nothing great was ever achieved without enthusiasm." RWE "Circles," *Essays, First Series*

"It takes years to write a book..." Annie Dillard, *The Writing Life*, 1990, Harper Perennial

Mary Rotch: "the dissent of all mankind cannot shake, and..." *The Selected Lectures of Ralph Waldo Emerson*, Edited by Ronald A. Bosco and Joel Myerson, 2005, University of Georgia Press, p. 353 ("The Rule of Life," 1867-1871)

Tilling Your Plot of Ground

"what you can get of moral or intellectual excellence out of this little plot of ground you call yourself...is your portion." RWE Ralph L. Rusk, *The Life of Ralph Waldo Emerson*, 1949, Charles Scribner's Sons, p.158 (Early Sermon)

"Can you...sail a ship through the Narrows..." RWE *Emerson in His Journals*, Selected and Ed. by Joel Porte, 1982, The Belknap Press of Harvard, p. 355 (May, 1846)

"The writer must live & die by his writing..." RWE *Emerson in His Journals*, Selected and Ed. by Joel Porte, 1982, The Belknap Press of Harvard University, p. 356 (May, 1846)

"I must do what I shall perish if I cannot do." RWE *The Selected Lectures of Ralph Waldo Emerson*, Edited by Ronald A. Bosco and Joel Myerson, 2005, University of Georgia Press, p. 84, ("The Poet" 1841-1842)

"He must embrace solitude as a bride..." RWE "Literary Ethics" 1838

"The paradox which confronts every writer..." Vivian C. Hopkins, *Spires of Form: A Study of Emerson's Aesthetic Theory*, 1951, Harvard University Press, p.225

"If a man is inflamed...and heeds only this one dream, which holds him like an insanity" RWE "The Poet," *Essays, Second Series*

He "gave up any debate on the spirit of the times..." Ralph L. Rusk, *The Life of Ralph Waldo Emerson*, 1949, Charles Scribner's Sons, p.406

"A scholar defending the cause of slavery..." RWE Edward Waldo Emerson, *Emerson in Concord: A Memoir*, 1888, Houghton Mifflin Company, p. 83

"Emerson's interest in reform...was too far-reaching...to be readily inflamed..." O.W. Firkins, *Ralph Waldo Emerson*, 1915, Houghton Mifflin Company, p.169

"He is a revealer of things. Let him first learn the things. Let him not...omit the work to be done." RWE "Literary Ethics" 1838

"a beautiful, transparent soul" **(Thomas Carlyle)** Ralph L. Rusk, *The Life of Ralph Waldo Emerson*, 1949, Charles Scribner's Sons, p.195

"in constant obedience to the demands of his highest nature." Charles J. Woodbury, *Talks with Emerson*, first pub. 1890, Horizon Press NY, 1970, p.129

"whose being revolved on a center of integrity as a personal law unto itself." George Edward Woodberry, *Ralph Waldo Emerson*, 1907, The Macmillan Company, p. 1

"to supply the axis on which the frame of things turns." RWE *Representative Men*, "Goethe; or, The Writer"

"the iron must be of good quality, so the scholar... must first be a man." RWE Edward Waldo Emerson, *Emerson in Concord: A Memoir*, 1888, Houghton Mifflin, p. 215

"his works are all one single attack on the vice of the age, moral cowardice..." John Jay Chapman, "Emerson," *Emerson and Other Essays*, 1898, NY Scribner's Sons

"His eloquence in affirming that in building character..." John McAleer, *Ralph Waldo Emerson: Days of Encounter*, 1984, Little Brown & Co., p. xii, xiii

"What he taught others to be, he was himself." Oliver Wendell Holmes, *Ralph Waldo Emerson*, 1885, Houghton Mifflin and Company, p.421

"Character pleads louder than art." Gay Wilson Allen, *Waldo Emerson: A Biography*, 1981, Viking Press New York, p. 51

"he had become the conscience of the nation — at least in the North and West." Gay Wilson Allen, *Waldo Emerson: A Biography*, 1981, Viking Press New York, p. 626

"While he lived his figure could be seen from Europe towering like Atlas..." John Jay Chapman, "Emerson," *Emerson and Other Essays*, 1898, Scribner's Sons

"a poor sterile Yankeeism" that remained barren unless "tasked" RWE Jonathan Bishop, *Emerson on the Soul*, 1964, Harvard University Press, p. 186, (J.VIII.74)

"he studies in his sleep, in his walking, in his meals, in his pleasures." RWE *Emerson in His Journals*, Selected and Edited by Joel Porte, 1982, The Belknap Press of Harvard University, p.346 (May 1846)

"He almost always refused offers to ride in a carriage..." Edward Waldo Emerson, *Emerson in Concord: A Memoir*, 1888, Houghton Mifflin Co. p. 156

Word by Word

John Casey story, "Master Class" by Parker Bauer, *The Weekly Standard*, Dec. 29, 2014

"The scholar is bound to stand for all the virtues and all the liberties" RWE Edward Waldo Emerson, *Emerson in Concord: A Memoir*, 1888, Houghton Mifflin Co., p.84

"Every writer is a skater..." RWE John McAleer, *Ralph Waldo Emerson: Days of Encounter*, 1984, Little Brown & Co., p.5 (JMN, XI, 195)

Nadine Gordimer quote, Nobel Lecture: Writing and Being, December 1991

"The Soul's Emphasis is Always Right"

"The Soul's Emphasis is always right." **RWE** "Spiritual Laws," *Essays, First Series*

"by putting your ear close to the soul, learn always the true way." **RWE** Lawrence Buell, *Emerson*, 2003, Belknap Press of Harvard University, p. 73 (JMN, 4:264)

"Every man has...an original impulse, by which nature contrives to get the work of the world done." Stephen E. Whicher, *Freedom and Fate: An Inner Life of Ralph Waldo Emerson*, 1953, University of Pennsylvania Press, p. 162

"Knowledge is the knowing that we cannot know." **RWE** *Representative Men*: "Montaigne; or, The Skeptic"

"He is a philosopher, a scholar...with a mind surpassing mine..." **RWE** Ralph L. Rusk, *The Life of Ralph Waldo Emerson*, 1949, Charles Scribner's Sons, p. 122

"in certain moments I have known that I existed directly from God..." **RWE** Richard Geldard, *The Spiritual Teachings of Ralph Waldo Emerson*, 2001, Lindisfarne Books, p. 60 (JMN, V. 337)

"Internal evidence outweighs all others to the inner man." **RWE** Gay Wilson Allen, *Waldo Emerson: A Biography*, 1981, Viking Press, p.163 (Journal, Dec. 11, 1830)

"Belief consists in accepting the affirmations of the soul; unbelief in denying them." **RWE** *Representative Men*, "Montaigne; or, The Skeptic"

"The soul is the perceiver and revealer of truth." **RWE** "The Over-Soul," *Essays, First Series*

"Why should not we also enjoy an original relation to the universe?" **RWE** *Nature*

"he was perhaps the most sweeping, the most fearless..." O.W. Firkins, *Ralph Waldo Emerson*, 1915, Houghton Mifflin Company, p.343

"It would be more exact to say that he overrated the *preponderance* of good." O.W. Firkins, *Ralph Waldo Emerson*, 1915, Houghton Mifflin Company, p.348

"always held that lower beliefs...were sure to give way...when higher ones were given." Edward Waldo Emerson, *Emerson in Concord: A Memoir*, 1888, Houghton Mifflin Co., p. 170

"because there is so much of his nature which is unlawfully withholden from him." John Dewey, "Emerson: The Philosopher of Democracy," read at the Emerson Memorial Meeting, University of Chicago, Mary 25, 1903, *International Journal of Ethics*, vol. 13, no. 4

"the individual...will take the moral path...given the gift of reflective thought." Richard G. Geldard, *God in Concord: Ralph Waldo Emerson's Awakening to the Infinite*, 1999, Larson Publications, p. 33

"I cannot find language of sufficient energy to convey my sense of the sacredness of private integrity." **RWE** Stephen E. Whicher, *Freedom and Fate: An Inner Life of Ralph Waldo Emerson*, 1953, University of Pennsylvania Press, p.78 ("Lecture on the Times"1841)

"sublime reliance on the simple force of truth." Stephen E. Whicher, *Freedom and Fate: An Inner Life of Ralph Waldo Emerson*, 1953, University of Pennsylvania Press, p.66 (Early Lecture, "Martin Luther")

"The soul looketh steadily forwards..." RWE "The Over-Soul," *Essays, First Series*

"genius looks forward" RWE "The American Scholar" 1837

"Genius is the activity which repairs the decay of things." RWE "The Poet" *Essays, Second Series*

"All things proceed out of the same spirit, and all things conspire with it..." RWE "Divinity School Address" 1838

"The highest and truest utterances of the poet are not his." RWE Charles J. Woodbury, *Talks with Emerson* (1890) 1970, Horizon Press NY, p. 35

"He knows that he did not make his thought..." RWE Edward Waldo Emerson, *Emerson in Concord: A Memoir*, 1888, Houghton Mifflin Company, p. 242

"A breath of will blows eternally through the universe of souls in the direction of the Right and Necessary." RWE Jay William Hudson, "The Religion of Emerson," *The Sewanee Review*, vol. 28, Apr. 1, 1920 ("Fate" 1860)

"All loss, all pain, is particular; the universe remains to the heart unhurt." RWE "Spiritual Laws," *Essays, First Series*

"All nature is the rapid efflux of goodness executing and organizing itself." RWE "Circles," ***Essays, First Series***

"The office of the scholar is to cheer, to raise, and to guide men..." RWE "The American Scholar" 1837

"Believe in magnetism, not in needles!" RWE Robert D. Richardson, Jr., *Emerson: Mind on Fire*, 1995, University of California Press, p. 4 (Journal, 1845)

"no ray of light, no pulse of good, is ever lost" RWE James Elliot Cabot, *A Memoir of Ralph Waldo Emerson*, 1887, Houghton Mifflin, p.565 ("Spirit of the Age" 1850)

"We know truth...as we know when we are awake that we are awake." RWE "The Over-Soul," *Essays, First Series*

"the all-consuming virtue which we vainly dodge and postpone, but which must be met and obeyed at last, if we wish to be substance, and not accidents." RWE James Elliot Cabot, *A Memoir of Ralph Waldo Emerson*, 1887, Houghton Mifflin, p.422

Aim High

"Lift your aims!" "Always do what you're afraid to do!" "Be generous and great..." Edward Waldo Emerson, *Emerson in Concord: A Memoir*, 1888, Houghton Mifflin Company, p.10,21

"An innavigable sea washes with silent waves between us and the things we aim at..." RWE "Experience," *Essays, Second Series*

"Every book is a quotation ..." RWE *Representative Men*, "Plato; or, The Philosopher"

"No great men are original." RWE *Representative Men*, "Shakespeare; or, The Poet"

"The power which they communicate is not theirs..." RWE *Representative Men*, "The Uses of Great Men"

The greatest genius is the most indebted man." RWE *Representative Men*, "Shakespeare; or, The Poet" "an incandescence not quite like anything else in literature" Stephen E. Whicher, *Selections from Ralph Waldo Emerson: An Organic Anthology*, 1957, Houghton Mifflin Co., p 410

"an indefinable something which flows out and over you like a flood of light." (Walt Whitman) Lawrence Buell, *Emerson*, 2003, Belknap Press of Harvard University, p. 320

"The best part of Emersonianism is, it breeds the giant that destroys itself..." Walt Whitman, "Emerson's Books (The Shadows of Them)" (1880) *Ralph Waldo Emerson, Bloom's Classic Critical Views*, Edited and Introduced by Harold Bloom, 2008, Infobase Publishing, p.68

"invites you to kill him off... makes him one of the most un-usual authority figures in the history of western culture." Lawrence Buell, *Emerson*, 2003, Belknap Press of Harvard University, p. 292

"We wish to hold these fellow minds as mirrors before ourselves to learn the deepest secret of our capacity" RWE Stephen E. Whicher, *Freedom and Fate: An Inner Life of Ralph Waldo Emerson*, 1953, University of Pennsylvania Press, p. 65 (Early Lecture: "George Fox")

"The best minds, who love truth for its own sake...do not label or stamp it with any man's name, for it is theirs long beforehand. It is theirs from eternity." RWE "The Over-Soul" *Essays, First Series*

"Were not the words that...brought the blood to your cheeks...Was it not truth that you knew before?" RWE *Selections from Ralph Waldo Emerson: An Organic Anthology*, Edited by Stephen E. Whicher, 1957, Houghton Mifflin Co., p. 9 (Oct. 27, 1831)

"This one fact the world hates, that the soul becomes." RWE "Self-Reliance," *Essays, First Series*

"So all that is said of the wise man...describes to each reader his own idea, describes his unattained but attainable self" RWE "History" *Essays, First Series*

"Every man is a new and incalculable power" RWE George Kateb, *Emerson and Self-Reliance*, 1995, Sage Publications, p.28 (Introductory, "The Philosophy of History," Early Lectures)

"Prayer is the contemplation of the facts of life from the highest point of view." RWE "Self Reliance," *Essays, First Series*

"Women see better than men." RWE *Emerson in His Journals*, Selected and Edited by Joel Porte, 1982, The Belknap Press of Harvard, p.231 (Nov. 1839)

"Woman is the power of Civilization." RWE *The Selected Lectures of Ralph Waldo Emerson*, Edited by Ronald A. Bosco and Joel Myerson, 2005, University of Georgia Press, p.149 ("Address at the Woman's Rights Convention" 1855)

"Certainly all my points would be sooner carried..." RWE *Emerson in His Journals*, Selected and Edited by Joel Porte, 1982, The Belknap Press of Harvard University, p.463 (July-Oct 1855)

"In the last decade alone, nearly one thousand articles and books..." Joel Myerson, *A Historical Guide to Ralph Waldo Emerson*, 2000, Oxford University Press, p. 3

"He will be found true by those Americans who know where to look..." Joel Porte, *Representative Man: Ralph Waldo Emerson in His Time*, 1979, New York Oxford University Press, p.325

"**principal architect of American culture**" Ronald A. Bosco, "A Brief Biography," *A Historical Guide to Ralph Waldo Emerson*, Edited by Joel Myerson, 2000, N.Y. Oxford University Press, p. 10

"**that part of America he created will cease to exist.**" Ronald A. Bosco, "We Find What We Seek: Emerson and His Biographers," *A Historical Guide to Ralph Waldo Emerson*, Edited by Joel Myerson, 2000, N.Y. Oxford University Press, p. 287

"**the life of our world may now depend on our grasping...**" Jacob Needleman, Introduction, *The Spiritual Emerson*, 2008, Penguin Group (USA) Inc.

"**Here was a man built to exert a rare influence upon a certain kind of highly sensitive...**" O.W. Firkins, *Ralph Waldo Emerson*, 1915, Houghton Mifflin Co., p.372

"**All literature is yet to be written. Poetry has scarce chanted its first song... Religion is yet to be settled on its fast foundations in the breast of man...**" RWE "Literary Ethics" 1838

"**What Plato has thought, he may think; what a saint has felt, he may feel; what at any time has befallen any man, he can understand.**" RWE "History," *Essays, First Series*

"**Build therefore your own world! RWE** *Nature*

The Process is the Prize

"**Colleges...have their indispensable office...set the hearts of their youth on flame.**" RWE "The American Scholar" 1837

"**by taking seedlings in a 'state of amelioration'...Mr. Emerson found...**" Edward Waldo Emerson, *Emerson in Concord: A Memoir*, 1888, Houghton Mifflin Company, p.131

"**the right and healthy state of every man...**" RWE Richard Geldard, *The Spiritual Teachings of Ralph Waldo Emerson*, 2001, Lindisfarne Books, p.145 ("Courage")

"**he is a candidate for truth...and respects the highest law of his being**" RWE "Intellect" *Essays, First Series*

"**By doing his own work, he unfolds himself.**" RWE "Spiritual Laws," *Essays, First Series*

"**who chose to be rich by making his wants few**" RWE H. B. Van Wesep, *Seven Sages: The Story of American Philosophy*, 1960, David McKay Co., p.104 (Emerson's Thoreau eulogy, 1862)

"**in the rambles of last night's talk with Henry [Thoreau]...**" RWE *Ralph Waldo Emerson*, Edited by Richard Poirier, 1990, Oxford University Press

"**in the sedulous inquiry, day after day, year after year...**" RWE "Literary Ethics" 1838

"**He is one, who...breathes and lives on...illustrious thoughts.**" RWE "The American Scholar" 1837 "to find the journey's end in every step of the road" RWE "Experience," *Essays, Second Series*

"Expression is prosperity." RWE *The Selected Lectures of Ralph Waldo Emerson*, Edited by Ronald A. Bosco and Joel Myerson, 2005, University of Georgia Press, p. 353 ("The Poet" 1841-1842)

"with the same mixture of mystery and calculation..." Vivian C. Hopkins, *Spires of Form: A Study of Emerson's Aesthetic Theory*, 1951, Harvard University Press, p.74

"Let a man learn...that he is here, not to work, but to be worked upon..." RWE *Representative Men*: "Montaigne; or, The Skeptic"

"We are always getting ready to live, but never living." RWE *The Heart of Emerson's Journals*, Edited by Bliss Perry, 1909, Houghton Mifflin Co., p.84 (April 1834)

"He is...exercising the highest functions of human nature." RWE "The American Scholar" 1837

"You will hear, that the first duty is to get land and money, place and name...to be its tongue to the heart of man..." RWE "Literary Ethics" 1838

Photography

Cover ...... Pixabay, Wendy Corniquet, WenPhotos
Emerson quote .... Unsplash, Nitish Kadam
Emerson photo .... photograph taken in 1847
Table of Contents .... Unsplash, Peter Aschoff
The Yearning to Write ... Unsplash, Sebastian Unrau
Page 4 .... Pixabay, Skeeze
Page 8 .... Pixabay, "esiul"
Page 12 .... Pixabay, Gerd Altmann
Page 26 .... Pixabay, Brigitte Werner
Page 40 .... Pixabay, Picography
Page 54 .... Pixabay, "Gotti1979"
Page 66 .... Pixabay, "perlaperla"
Page 76 .... Unsplash, Aaron Burden
Page 86 .... Pixabay, Andrew Montgomery
Page 98 .... Pixabay, "zhouhao509"
Page 112 .... Pixabay, "Bergadder"
Page 124 .... Pixabay, Anja Osenberg
Page 134 .... Pixabay, Skeeze
Page 144 .... Pixabay, "Inspired Images"
Page 158 .... Pixabay, Greg Krycinski
Page 160 ... Pixabay, Wendy Corniquet, WenPhotos
Page 180 .... Unsplash, Blake Richard Verdoorn

Thank you for sharing, and for your artistry.

Gleam of Light Press
GleamOfLightPress.com